FOR THE LOVE OF
RADIO 4

FOR THE LOVE OF
RADIO 4

AN UNOFFICIAL COMPANION

CAROLINE HODGSON

summersdale

CONTENTS

Foreword..7

Radio 4 in Facts and Figures..9

Introduction..27

The Home Service and Radio 4: A Brief History....................30

Radio 4 Now..46

And Now for the News..61

Cheers and Tears..80

Talking Politics – Radio 4's Relationship with Westminster....83

Today..93

Drama and Readings..100

The Archers..116

Comedy and Light Entertainment..124

I'm Sorry I Haven't a Clue..138

Arts, Culture and History..146

Desert Island Discs..168

Listener-focused Programming..174

Women on Radio 4..183

Woman's Hour..186

Science and Nature..192

Gardeners' Question Time..202

Religion and Ethics..208

Sport on 4..222

Test Match Special..225

Letter from America..231

Select Bibliography..234

Acknowledgements..235

FOREWORD

I was brought up on a delicious diet of BBC Radio 4. Other people may have breathed plain air but for us the air was heavily laden with Radio 4 classics such as *Woman's Hour*, *The Archers*, *Today*, *Just a Minute*, *Letter from America*, *World at One*... and of course, *Gardeners' Question Time*! I think it would be fair to say that I inherited this addiction with enthusiasm. After all who wouldn't delight in the opportunity to soak up information, humour and thought-provoking programmes whilst going about one's daily life?

So it was with a good deal of interest that I investigated *For the Love of Radio 4: An Unofficial Companion*. To my relief and pleasure I can confirm that this little book is packed to bursting with fascinating facts about everything from wavelengths where the station can be heard to presenters' thoughts and anecdotes galore. It traces the development, background and evolution of many of my favourite programmes, yours too I expect. Delve a little deeper and more facts, figures and comment in the book make listening to those favourite programmes even better. After all, having a good friend is one thing but being privileged to knowledge of that friend's innermost thoughts, workings and relationships puts your friendship on an even higher level.

For the Love of Radio 4 is a book to read at any time, in any place, all in one go or, I think better still, to delve into and savour as the mood takes you. Unoffical Companion it may be, but it is definitely one for my bookshelf, bedside or bag.

Pippa Greenwood

RADIO 4 IN FACTS AND FIGURES

RADIO 4'S REMIT

The remit of Radio 4 is to be a mixed speech service, offering in-depth news and current affairs and a wide range of other speech output including drama, readings, comedy, factual and magazine programmes.

Its stated aim is to appeal to listeners seeking intelligent programmes in many genres which inform, educate and entertain.

RADIO 4'S REACH

92.4–94.6 FM	Most of Britain, parts of Ireland and northern France
198 long wave (LW)	Throughout the UK, parts of northern Europe and the Atlantic area north of the Azores
Medium wave (MW)	Limited areas (see below)
DAB & digital TV	Freeview, Freesat, Sky, Virgin Media and online

Radio 4 is available on medium wave in certain locations:

Aberdeen	1449 MW
Belfast	720 MW
Carlisle	1485 MW
Cornwall	756 MW
Enniskillen	774 MW
London	720 MW
Londonderry	720 MW
Newcastle	603 MW
Plymouth	774 MW

SOME TERMS AND ABBREVIATIONS

FM = frequency modulation
DAB = Digital Audio Broadcasting
Hz = hertz, a unit of frequency of electrical vibrations (1 hertz = one cycle per second)
KHz = kilohertz (1,000 cycles per second)

A TYPICAL WEEKDAY SCHEDULE ON RADIO 4

This sample schedule is taken from May/June 2014. Some series will have a limited run and may or may not be recommissioned. Other strands, such as *Woman's Hour* and *Today*, are fixed in the schedule.

1 a.m.	Simulcast from the BBC World Service
5.20 a.m.	*Shipping Forecast*
5.30 a.m.	*News Briefing*
5.43 a.m.	*Prayer for the Day*
5.45 a.m.	*Farming Today*
5.56 a.m.	Weather

5.58 a.m.	*Tweet of the Day*
6 a.m.	*Today*, including *Thought for the Day*
9 a.m.	The schedule here is determined by the day of the week, with certain 'fixtures' each day, depending on the season:
	Monday – *Start the Week*
	Tuesday – *The Life Scientific*, followed by *One to One*
	Wednesday – *Midweek*
	Thursday – *In Our Time*
	Friday – *Desert Island Discs*
9.45 a.m.	*Book of the Week*
10 a.m.	*Woman's Hour*
10.45 a.m.	*15-minute Drama*
11 a.m.	Monday – *D-Day Dames*, followed by *Rudy's Rare Records*
	Tuesday – *Shared Planet*, followed by *Tales from the Stave*
	Wednesday – *Laurence Llewelyn-Bowen's Primary Colours*, followed by *When the Dog Dies*
	Thursday – *From Our Own Correspondent*, followed by *Body and Soul*
	Friday – *D-Day: A Family Affair*, followed by *Polyoaks*
Midday	*You and Yours*
12.57 p.m.	Weather
1 p.m.	*World at One*
1.45 p.m.	*Britain at Sea*
2 p.m.	*The Archers*
2.15 p.m.	*Afternoon Drama*
3 p.m.	Monday – *Round Britain Quiz*, followed by the *Food Programme*
	Tuesday – *The Kitchen Cabinet*, followed by *Shared Experience*

	Wednesday – *Money Box Live*, followed by *All in the Mind*
	Thursday – *Ramblings*, followed by *Open Book* or *Bookclub*
	Friday – *Gardeners' Question Time*, followed by *Skylines*
4 p.m.	Monday – *Burrell's Bequest*, followed by *Beyond Belief*
	Tuesday – *Law in Action*, followed by *A Good Read*
	Wednesday – *Thinking Allowed*, followed by *The Media Show*
	Thursday – *The Film Programme*, followed by *Inside Science*
	Friday – *Last Word*, followed by *More or Less* and *The Listening Project*
5 p.m.	*PM*
6 p.m.	*Six O'Clock News*
6.30 p.m.	The comedy half-hour. Fixtures include:
	Monday – *Just a Minute*, *I'm Sorry I Haven't a Clue* or *The Unbelievable Truth*
	Friday – *The Now Show*, *The News Quiz*
7 p.m.	*The Archers*
7.15 p.m.	*Front Row*
7.45 p.m.	*15-minute Drama*
8 p.m.	Monday – *Women at War*, followed by *Analysis*
	Tuesday – *File on 4*, followed by *In Touch*
	Wednesday – *Fit for Purpose*, followed by *Four Thought*
	Thursday – *The Report*, followed by *In Business* or *The Bottom Line*
	Friday – *Any Questions?* followed by *A Point of View*

9 p.m.	Monday – *Is Journalism Healthy?* followed by *Start the Week*
	Tuesday – *All in the Mind*, followed by *The Life Scientific*
	Wednesday – *Frontiers*, followed by *Midweek*
	Thursday – *Inside Science*, followed by *In Our Time*
	Friday – *Britain at Sea* omnibus
9.58 p.m.	Weather
10 p.m.	*The World Tonight*
10.45 p.m.	*Book at Bedtime*
11 p.m.	Monday – *The Human Zoo*, followed by *Lives in a Landscape*
	Tuesday – *Act Your Age*, followed by *Lives in a Landscape*
	Wednesday – *Mission Improbable,* followed by *I Regress* and *Today in Parliament* (when Parliament is sitting)
	Thursday – *Blocked*, followed by *Today in Parliament*
	Friday – *A Good Read*, followed by *Today in Parliament* and *The Listening Project*
Midnight	*Midnight News*
12.30 a.m.	*Book of the Week*
12.48 a.m.	*Shipping Forecast*

A news bulletin is broadcast on the hour every hour. If a programme is about to start it will be a two-minute summary, or it could be a longer bulletin if it leads into a current affairs programme.

A TYPICAL SATURDAY SCHEDULE

5.45 a.m.	*iPM*
6 a.m.	*News and Papers*
6.07 a.m.	*Ramblings*
6.30 a.m.	*Farming Today*
7 a.m.	*Today*
9 a.m.	*Saturday Live*
10.30 a.m.	*The Kitchen Cabinet*
11 a.m.	*Week in Westminster*
11.30 a.m.	*From Our Own Correspondent*
Midday	*Money Box*
12.30 p.m.	Repeat of the Friday 6.30 p.m. comedy
1 p.m.	News
1.10 p.m.	*Any Questions?*
2 p.m.	*Any Answers?*
2.30 p.m.	*Saturday Drama*
4 p.m.	*Weekend Woman's Hour*
5 p.m.	*Saturday PM*
5.30 p.m.	*The Bottom Line*
5.54 p.m.	*Shipping Forecast*, Weather and *Six O'Clock News*
6.15 p.m.	*Loose Ends*
7 p.m.	*From Fact to Fiction*
7.15 p.m.	*Saturday Review*
8 p.m.	*Archive on 4*
9 p.m.	*Classic Serial*
10 p.m.	News and Weather
10.15 p.m.	*Moral Maze*
11 p.m.	*Round Britain Quiz*
11.30 p.m.	*Poetry Please*

A TYPICAL SUNDAY SCHEDULE

5.43 a.m.	*Bells on Sunday*
5.45 a.m.	*Four Thought*
6.05 a.m.	*Something Understood*
6.35 a.m.	*On Your Farm*
7 a.m.	*News and Papers*
7.10 a.m.	*Sunday*
7.55 a.m.	*Radio 4 Appeal*
8 a.m.	*News and Papers*
8.10 a.m.	*Sunday Worship*
8.48 a.m.	*A Point of View*
8.58 a.m.	*Tweet of the Day*
9 a.m.	*Broadcasting House*
10 a.m.	*The Archers* omnibus
11.15 a.m.	*Desert Island Discs*
Midday	Repeat of the Monday 6.30 p.m. comedy
12.32 p.m.	*Food Programme*
1 p.m.	*The World This Weekend*
1.30 p.m.	*Tales from the Stave*
2 p.m.	*Gardeners' Question Time*
2.45 p.m.	*The Listening Project* omnibus
3 p.m.	*Classic Serial*
4 p.m.	*Open Book* or *Bookclub*
4.30 p.m.	*Poetry Please*
5 p.m.	*File on 4*
5.40 p.m.	*From Fact to Fiction*
5.54 p.m.	*Shipping Forecast,* Weather and *Six O'Clock News*
6.15 p.m.	*Pick of the Week*
7 p.m.	*The Archers*
7.15 p.m.	*Blofeld and Baxter*
8 p.m.	*More or Less*
8.30 p.m.	*Last Word*

9 p.m.	*Money Box*
9.26 p.m.	*Radio 4 Appeal*
9.30 p.m.	*Analysis*
10 p.m.	*Westminster Hour*
10.45 p.m.	*What the Papers Say*
11 p.m.	*The Film Programme*
11.30 p.m.	*Something Understood*

Note: DAB radio and BBC iPlayer follow the Radio 4 FM schedule.

LONG-WAVE WEEKDAY VARIATIONS

When Parliament is sitting, *Yesterday in Parliament* airs on LW at 8.30 a.m., while FM listeners are hearing the last half-hour of *Today*.

At 9.45 a.m. Radio 4 LW broadcasts the *Daily Service*, while FM is broadcasting *Book of the Week*.

At midday, before the start of *You and Yours*, FM has a four-minute news bulletin while on LW you will hear the headlines followed by the *Shipping Forecast*.

LW leaves *PM* at 5.54 p.m., again to make room for the *Shipping Forecast*.

NUMBER CRUNCHING – OUR RADIO-LISTENING HABITS IN THE UK

48.1 million	The number of adults of 15+ who tune into their radios each week.
90 per cent	How that equates to a percentage of the adult UK population.
1.04 billion	The total average number of weekly hours spent listening to radio.

21.5	The number of hours the average radio listener tunes in per week.
27.1 million	People who now tune in via a digitally enabled receiver (DAB, DTV, online).
51 per cent	The same figure as a percentage of the adult UK population.
26 million	Digital listeners in 2013.

Figures from RAJAR (Radio Joint Audience Research) for the first quarter of 2014.

NATIONAL WEEKLY LISTENING FIGURES

Today – 7.06 million
The Archers – 4.92 million
PM – 4 million
Woman's Hour – 3.68 million
Book of the Week – 3.15 million
World at One – 3.1 million
Today on Saturday – 3.1 million
Desert Island Discs – 2.99 million
Afternoon Drama – 2.66 million
Just a Minute – 2.42 million
Front Row – 2.21 million
Broadcasting House – 1.9 million
Gardeners' Question Time – 1.53 million
Book at Bedtime – 1.26 million
Money Box – 1.2 million

Figures from RAJAR (Radio Joint Audience Research) for the first quarter of 2014.

A TIMELINE OF THE HOME SERVICE

1922   The British government licenses the British Broadcasting Company.

Daily broadcasting from the London transmitter begins in November, followed by Birmingham, Manchester and Newcastle.

John Reith is appointed General Manager.

1923   First BBC outside broadcast takes place.

Savoy Hill becomes the BBC's headquarters.

The *Radio Times* is first published.

1924   The BBC's first long-wave transmitter is opened at Chelmsford (transferred to Daventry a year later).

The Greenwich and Big Ben time signals ('pips and bongs') are introduced.

1926   National radio transmission begins on the National Programme.

Reith successfully petitions the government to be allowed to broadcast more news during the General Strike.

1927   The British Broadcasting Company becomes a corporation and is granted a ten-year Royal Charter.

First short-wave broadcasts to Europe from Chelmsford.

Reith becomes Director General.

First sports broadcasts.

The Proms becomes the BBC Proms, and is broadcast for the first time from the Albert Hall.

1930   The regional system of broadcasting begins. The National Programme now runs alongside the Regional Programme, which includes programmes originating in six regions.

1931   Businessman, entrepreneur and wireless fanatic Leonard Plugge launches the International Broadcasting Company as a commercial rival to the BBC. He buys airtime from

French radio stations and starts broadcasting English-language programmes from France.

1932   The BBC moves from Savoy Hill to Broadcasting House. Launch of the Empire Service.

1934   The Droitwich transmitter starts broadcasting the National Programme.

1937   A programme called *Farming Today* is first introduced on BBC Radio.

1940   Princess Elizabeth (then aged fourteen) and Princess Margaret address the children of the Empire on the Empire Service.

       A bomb explodes at Broadcasting House, killing seven.

1941   Yorkshireman Wilfred Pickles becomes the first newsreader on the Home Service with a regional accent.

1942   Vic Oliver is Roy Plomley's first castaway on *Desert Island Discs*.

1945   The Light Programme is launched.

       Regional broadcasting resumes after the war.

1946   The Third Programme is launched.

       On the Light Programme, *Woman's Hour* becomes the first radio programme specifically aimed at women.

       Alistair Cooke broadcasts his first *Letter from America* on the Home Service (it would run until Cooke's death in 2004).

       Down Your Way is launched on the Home Service.

1947   The *Gardeners' Question Time* format first appears as *How Does Your Garden Grow?* in the BBC North region.

1948   *Any Questions?* is first broadcast in the BBC West region.

1949   *Book at Bedtime* is introduced.

1950   *The Archers* is first broadcast on the Light Programme.

1953 *Brain of Britain* first transmitted as an insert in *What Do You Know?*

1954 A radio licence costs £1.

1955 *From Our Own Correspondent* is launched.

1957 *Today* is first broadcast as a light-hearted look at the news.

1964 Frank Gillard abolishes the Features Department.

1965 The cost of a radio licence is increased to £1 and 5 shillings.

  World at One (*WATO*) is launched.

A TIMELINE OF RADIO 4

1967 The Home Service becomes Radio 4 on 30 September.

  Launch of *Just a Minute*.

  Programmes are broadcast on Sunday morning for the first time.

1968 *The World Tonight* first airs.

1970 New programmes introduced include *PM*, *Start the Week*, *Week Ending* (until 1998) and *You and Yours*.

  It's Your Line (until 1976), fronted by Robin Day, is Radio 4's first phone-in programme.

  Thought for the Day is introduced.

  First transmission of *Analysis*, a programme which examines 'the ideas and forces which shape public policy in Britain and abroad'.

1972 Humphrey Lyttelton first gives the panel silly things to do on *I'm Sorry I Haven't a Clue*.

1973 Arts show *Kaleidoscope* launched (until 1998).

  Woman's Hour is transferred from Radio 2 to Radio 4 in the afternoons.

  Checkpoint with Roger Cook (until 1985) (became *Face the Facts*).

1974   Weekly chat show *Wogan's World* is launched.
        Launch of *Stop the Week* with Robert Robinson (until 1992).
        After budget cuts, Radio 3 and Radio 4 have to share programming on Saturday afternoons.
1977   Launch of *Money Box*, *Does He Take Sugar?* (until 1998), *File on 4* and *The News Quiz*.
1978   *The Hitchhiker's Guide to the Galaxy* is broadcast.
        Radio 4 inherits the *Shipping Forecast* from the Met Office.
        Radio 4 moves to long wave.
        Fritz Spiegl is commissioned to produce the Radio 4 theme tune – an arrangement of traditional airs that highlight Radio 4 as a service encompassing the whole of Britain.
1979   The launch of *Feedback*.
        The *Food Programme* first airs, founded by Derek Cooper.
1981   *The Lord of the Rings* is broadcast for the first time.
1982   *Adrian Mole* hits the airwaves.
        Listen with Mother is scrapped after thirty-two years, despite protests from high-profile fans including Alan Ayckbourn, Barbara Cartland, John Cleese, Glenda Jackson and Harry Secombe.
1985   *After Henry* is broadcast on Radio 4 (until 1989).
        Roy Plomley dies and Michael Parkinson takes over *Desert Island Discs*.
1986   *Pick of the Week* is moved from Saturday to Sunday and its slot is filled by *Loose Ends*, hosted by Ned Sherrin.
1988   Sue Lawley takes over *Desert Island Discs* from Michael Parkinson.
1990   The unexpurgated *Lady Chatterley's Lover* is featured on *Book at Bedtime*.
1991   Radio 4 moves to FM from long wave.

Woman's Hour is moved from the afternoon to a 10.30 a.m. slot.

1992   Discussions start about 'producer choice' – outsourcing programmes to independent producers.

Threats to scrap long wave lead to the launch of the Save Radio 4 Long Wave campaign.

1993   *Sunday Outing* is Radio 4's first dedicated gay and lesbian programme.

1994   BBC Radio 5 Live is launched.

The *Gardeners' Question Time* panel defects to Classic FM.

1995   The BBC begins the world's first digital audio broadcasting (DAB) transmissions.

1997   Radio 4's news staff move to BBC Television Centre to combine with television news.

1998   Under James Boyle's extensive schedule changes, *Home Truths* is launched (until John Peel's death in 2004).

Front Row replaces *Kaleidoscope*.

In Our Time is introduced, presented by Melvyn Bragg.

Broadcasting House first airs.

The 6.30 p.m. comedy slot is created.

1999   First commercial DAB radio service launched.

2000   Start of *Dead Ringers* (until 2007 – reintroduced in 2014).

2001   *Go4It* – a children's magazine programme – is introduced on Sunday evenings (until 2009).

2002   BBC Radio 7 is launched.

2003   Andrew Gilligan's report on the *Today* programme about the 'sexed-up' dossier on Iraqi weapons of mass destruction. Suicide of weapons expert Dr David Kelly.

2004   Publication of the Hutton Report into Dr Kelly's death.

2006   Kirsty Young replaces Sue Lawley on *Desert Island Discs*.

Saturday Live occupies the slot previously held by *Home Truths*.

Fritz Spiegl's theme tune is axed.

2007   Clive Anderson takes over *Loose Ends* after Ned Sherrin's death the previous year.

2008   Humphrey Lyttleton's illness and subsequent death in April leaves the *I'm Sorry I Haven't a Clue* team without silly things to do for a while. Rob Brydon and others step into the breach.

The Media Show replaces *The Message*.

2010   *A History of the World in 100 Objects* is broadcast.

2011   Radio 7 is relaunched as Radio 4 Extra.

2013   With the closure of BBC Television Centre in London, the move of BBC News staff to Broadcasting House is complete.

2014   Character Invasion Day on 29 March sees the Vicar of Dibley reading *Thought for the Day*, and *Tweet of the Day* coming from Big Bird.

BROADCASTING BASES

RADIO 4 PROGRAMMES CURRENTLY BROADCAST FROM SALFORD

Archive on 4
Beyond Belief
Brain of Britain
Counterpoint
File on 4
Front Row (two programmes per week)
Moral Maze
Pick of the Week
Round Britain Quiz
Thought for the Day
Woman's Hour (one programme per week plus inserts)
You and Yours

RADIO 4 PROGRAMMES CURRENTLY BROADCAST FROM BIRMINGHAM

The Archers
Between Ourselves
Costing the Earth
Farming Today
Food and Farming Awards
Food Programme
On the Ropes
On Your Farm
Open Country
Ramblings

RADIO 4 PROGRAMMES CURRENTLY BROADCAST FROM BRISTOL

A Good Read
Any Answers?
Any Questions?
Great Lives
In Living Memory
Off the Page
Poetry Please
With Great Pleasure
Word of Mouth

RADIO 4 CONTROLLERS

Gerard Mansell	1965–1967 (Home Service), 1967–1969 (Radio 4)
Tony Whitby	1970–1975
Clare Lawson Dick	1975–1976
Ian McIntyre	1976–1978

Monica Sims	1978–1983
David Hatch	1983–1986
Michael Green	1986–1996
James Boyle	1996–2000
Helen Boaden	2000–2004
Mark Damazer	2004–2010
Gwyneth Williams	2010–present

BBC RADIO STATIONS

Radio 1
Radio 2
Radio 3
Radio 4
Radio 4 Extra
5 Live
5 Live Sports Extra
1Xtra
6 Music
Asian Network
World Service
Radio Cymru
Radio Scotland
Radio nan Gaidheal (the Gaelic-language station)
Radio Ulster/Foyle
Radio Wales
CBeebies Radio
BBC local stations

INTRODUCTION

> **"** *If I had a word running through me like a stick of rock it would be 'radio'. It might even be two words – 'BBC Radio'.* **"**
>
> **SANDI TOKSVIG**

You can bet your life that had Samuel Johnson been alive today, he would have been a Radio 4 stalwart, at the least contributing to and very probably fronting a number of its programmes (perhaps 'Boswell and I', or an *Excess Baggage* report from the Western Isles). And just possibly, he might have substituted 'Radio 4' for 'London' in his famous saying: 'When a man is tired of London, he is tired of life; for there is in London all that life can afford.'

Because all life is, indeed, to be found on Radio 4. It's hardly surprising, perhaps, given that an estimated 330,000 hours of material have been transmitted since 1967. To do it justice would take as long again, plus the time it would take to cover everything that goes on behind the scenes – the programmes, producers, presenters, politicians and public and, occasionally, political fallout. In other words, this book can survey only the tip of the great iceberg that is Radio 4.

Apart from the breadth and quality of its output, undoubtedly one of the things people value about Radio 4 is its companionship. In the chapter about *The Archers*, actress Alison Dowling (Elizabeth Pargetter) declares: 'my radio is like a best friend.' It's a sentiment you come across a lot when you talk to people about Radio 4 and what it means to them.

Like all good company, Radio 4 is undemanding. Here's a Twitter exchange which sums up the way in which many people listen to it:

Whatsit @mattwhatsit
I have no idea AT. ALL. what is going on in The Archers, I just like how it sounds as I'm cooking breakfast. I think Kate wants a baby?

Claire Davis @clairedavis45
@mattwhatsit I had the Archers on every week for 15 years and couldn't name any character or follow any story. It's just nice sounds.

SallyPC @SallyPC
@clairedavis45 @mattwhatsit I do the same with Test Match Special – no idea what the score is, just love the summer sounds!

That is not, however, to suggest that Radio 4 doesn't engage, entertain and enrich us when we fully tune into it. It is above all the station for the curious – people who want to know about life, the universe and everything in it.

Like all good companions, of course, it is capable of failure. For all that it has the world's best technicians, no radio station can function day and night for nigh on fifty years (over ninety if you count the Home Service) without a glitch. It is, after all, only human. But when we hear an unscheduled minute of silence, or a presenter having a fit of giggles, we love it all the more. Although the presenters and personalities are some of the most brilliant in their field, failure happens. And when it does, we just lap it up.

And that's another thing about Radio 4 – we all contribute to and shape it. You can bet your life that Jeremy Hardy never consciously came up with a ruse to sing badly on *I'm Sorry I Haven't a Clue*. If anything, he resisted singing with every fibre of his body (as you would, in his place). But when he had to sing, we picked up on just how woeful it really was, and it transformed into a feature of the show. Whether you're a presenter, producer, personality, panel member, in the studio audience or a listener at home, you are an organic part of the alchemy which, when it happens, creates pure radio gold.

THE HOME SERVICE
AND RADIO 4: A
BRIEF HISTORY

At midnight on 29 September 1967, BBC announcer David Dunhill signed off from the Home Service for the last time. At 6.35 a.m. the following morning, he said, Britain would wake up to BBC Radio 4. In his cut-glass accent, Dunhill likened the change to that of a bride on the eve of her wedding – she who would go on being the same person, he said, just with a new name.

PREHISTORY

It all started in 1922, when the BBC started its first daily radio service, broadcasting for a few hours a day. The first ten years – between the wars – were the Savoy Hill years, when the British Broadcasting Company, just off the Strand, had a gentleman's-club feel about it. The 'History of the BBC' website evokes this, with an image of contributors such as H. G. Wells and George Bernard Shaw being offered whisky and soda as they waited to go on air.

Although socially BBC Radio might have been rooted in an age of Edwardian protocol and manners, at the same time radio was a developing industry, full of self-made men. Radio technology had come on in leaps and bounds during World War One, and in these formative years everything was up for grabs. Nobody really knew the limitations or potential of radio, so to be part of this phenomenon wasn't dependent on your CV, experience or track record. Indeed, there was no such thing as a track record (although being a man was, of course, a prerequisite).

It is quite inconceivable, for example, that John Reith would be given a job today based on the interview he had on 13 December 1922 for the post of General Manager. As he recorded later in his diary, he was not asked many questions, and some of those he was asked he didn't know the meaning of!

This wasn't just a phenomenon of the very early years. In 1929 Val Gielgud was put in charge of radio drama despite never having directed a radio play himself. Later still, in the mid 1940s, the poet Louis MacNeice was experimenting wildly with drama in the Features Department, apparently getting away with it because it seems nobody quite knew what 'features' were.

You can imagine a modern-day Reith swotting up by doing background research the night before his interview, having been required to complete numerous forms in advance. Gielgud would simply never have got a look in (as a result of which Joe Orton might never have got his break), and MacNeice's Features Department would long ago have fallen prey to budget cuts.

Maybe it's right that things should be sharper, more efficient and professional – after all, there are the stakeholders to consider these days – but it's also true that without the chaos of the early days we wouldn't have the Radio 4 we have today, or anything resembling it.

66 *The fact is I hadn't the remotest idea as to what broadcasting was. I hadn't troubled to find out...* **99**

**JOHN REITH AFTER HIS INTERVIEW
WITH THE BBC, 1922**

A LITTLE **4** THOUGHT

As a form of communication, radio broadcasting was perceived to be an extension of the postal services, and the BBC was originally licensed through the General Post Office.

The British Broadcasting Company became a corporation in 1927, when it was granted a ten-year Royal Charter.

THE HOME SERVICE ON THE HOME FRONT

It was on the newly instated Home Service, on 3 September 1939, that Neville Chamberlain's famous, doom-laden words stopped the country in its tracks when he announced that 'this country is at war with Germany'.

Just two days previously, on 1 September, BBC Radio's two stations – the National Programme and the Regional Programme – had been merged to become the Home Service. This was a pragmatic move, in order to prevent enemy aircraft from using the Regional Programme's transmitters for navigating. With the synchronisation of the two frequencies it became impossible to broadcast to the regions. At the same time, because of fears of attacks on the capital, the regional studios started to be used for national broadcasting.

In 1939, for example, Clare Lawson Dick, who would later become Controller of Radio 4, was a clerical worker at the BBC's Registry in Wood Norton Hall in Worcestershire – the BBC's 'secret' location. Lawson Dick and other staff received instructions on what to do if the siren sounded. The memo read: 'If the alert is sounded, staff must run into the woods immediately and lie down. Preferably in pairs.'

66 *I have always enjoyed the 'dotty' side of the BBC.* **99**

CLARE LAWSON DICK, CONTROLLER OF RADIO 4, 1975–1976

A LITTLE **4** THOUGHT

In 1938, John Reith's last act at the BBC was to personally close down the National Programme at Droitwich before he signed the visitors' book and left. He recorded in his diary: 'All over.'

In the early days newsreaders were required to wear dinner jackets for the evening shift, while announcer Charles Lister recalls being severely censured for wearing yellow socks.

SENDING OUT SIGNALS – THE EMPIRE SERVICE AND EUROPEAN SERVICE

The Empire Service (later the Overseas Service and now the World Service) deserves a mention here because it was at the vanguard of the technological advances which would cascade throughout the whole of radio broadcasting.

The BBC Empire Service was a short-wave service launched in 1932, aimed principally at English speakers in the outposts of the British Empire. Initially, Reith had very low expectations of the Empire Service. In his opening address he said: 'Don't expect too much in the early days... The programmes will neither be very interesting nor very good.'

One of the first broadcasts was King George V's Christmas message – the first time a monarch's voice had been heard by millions of his subjects simultaneously. In his speech, the King addressed the 'men and women so cut off by the snows, the desert or the sea, that only voices out of the air can reach them'. As pre-recording technology was not sufficiently advanced, this address was read out five times as it was broadcast live to different parts of the world. By the end, as he would later record in his diary, he was 'very bored of it'.

At the start of World War Two, the BBC's only short-wave transmitting station for the Empire Service was at Daventry. The rapid expansion of overseas services soon necessitated the building of new sites: in Dorset (Rampisham), Devon (Start Point), Somerset (Clevedon), Cumbria (Skelton) and Shropshire (Woofferton). On the east coast a long-wave transmitter was built at Spurn Head to send signals to Germany.

In November 1939 the Empire Service was renamed the Overseas Service. The Forces Programme was launched in 1940, and the European Service in 1941. In addition, by the end of 1942, BBC Radio was broadcasting in all major European languages. Necessity really had, as the adage goes, become the mother of invention as far as radio communication was concerned.

> **66** *I knew that... there was... the BBC speaking calmly and authoritatively... about the weather, the news and the Empire.* **99**
> **ERIC LOMAX, THE RAILWAY MAN, 1995**

A LITTLE **4** THOUGHT

On 15 October 1940 Broadcasting House took a direct hit from a German bomb, killing seven people.

During the war, the European Service was involved in broadcasting secret messages to resistance fighters in Europe.

INFORMATION IS POWER – RECORDING THE WAR

Along with improvements in transmission technology, the other urgent challenge facing BBC Radio engineers was how to improve information-gathering.

Before 1930 the BBC had no viable means of recording sound. Even then, in 1930, the steel-tape technology of the Blattnerphone resulted in recordings which were capable of recording voice, but were not good enough quality for music. The spools were cumbersome and the editing process was essentially a soldering job that was time-consuming and hazardous – a broken tape could result in razor-edged steel snapping free and flying around the editing room.

The Blattnerphone was not remotely portable, so when BBC correspondents were sent to cover the war, they took with them 'Midget' discs that looked like old-fashioned record players.

By this time the Germans had already developed the Magnetophon, the archetype of the modern tape recorder, which used plastic-based tape. Editing was done using a razor blade and sticky tape. After the war, Allied engineers took captured Magnetophons home, and the electrical firm EMI developed the BTR/1 tape recorder from it.

A LITTLE **4** THOUGHT

Midget discs weighed about 30 pounds and recorded about 2 minutes' worth of material at 78 rpm.

An only slightly modified version of the BTR/1 tape recorder was still being used within the BBC as late as the 1970s.

These days, excluding World Service output and 'presentation' (what the announcers say), around 50 per cent of Radio 4's programming is broadcast live and 50 per cent is recorded.

SOMETHING FOR EVERYONE – THE POST-WAR YEARS

Regional programming was resumed after the war. In addition, the Forces Programme became the Light Programme (the forerunner of Radio 2), and the Third Programme (later Radio 3) was launched in 1946. This was the start of 'streaming' radio for individual tastes.

Television broadcasting had started in the United Kingdom in 1936, although BBC Television services were suspended between 1939 and 1946. After the war the nation started looking around for new diversions, and it's probably fair to say that the late 1940s and the 1950s were the wilderness years for radio. That's not to say that nothing happened on radio, but that the power and potential of the moving image had a kind of mesmerising effect upon the nation. The introduction of commercial channels in 1955 heralded the democratisation of broadcast communication, and created a hunger for consumer choice. Radio 'listening-in' parties were replaced by viewing parties, and any television-owning household in the street became a social hub for major events. When Elizabeth II's coronation was televised in 1953, it is estimated that 20.4 million adults (double the radio audience) watched it on 2.7 million television sets. It was the first time the television-viewing audience outnumbered the radio-listening audience.

At the same time, although television ownership was top of the aspiration list in many households, it was simply not an economic reality for many. Families still gathered around the radio of an evening, and during the 1950s and early 1960s the Light Programme, Home Service and Third Programme were steadily building up their schedules.

In 1946 Alistair Cooke broadcast his first *Letter from America*, and *Woman's Hour* became the first dedicated radio programme for women. It was also the year that *Down Your Way* was launched. Each week the presenter would visit a town, meet the people who lived there and play their choice of music – an 'out-and-about' format that shows just how portable radio had become since the days of the Midget.

The following year, 1947, saw the start of *Gardeners' Question Time* (then titled *How Does Your Garden Grow?*), while the 1950s brought *The Archers*, *Brain of Britain*, *From Our Own Correspondent* and the *Today* programme to the airwaves. Of course they were all very different in those days, but a modern Radio 4 listener transported back to the 1950s would very likely instantly recognise many of the programmes which still grace the Radio 4 airwaves.

A LITTLE **4** THOUGHT

Down Your Way ran until 1992, and its presenters included Richard Dimbleby, Franklin Engelmann and Brian Johnston. By the end it was generally agreed that its format had well and truly run out of steam, and in the 1980s Kenny Everett's saccharine spoof of it, 'Up Your Way', was presented by 'Verity Treacle'.

1967 AND ALL THAT

When Radio 4 was launched in 1967, under the auspices of Managing Director of BBC Radio Frank Gillard, it was alongside Radios 1, 2 and 3. Radio 1 was the hip and groovy new kid on the block, while Radio 2 took over from the Light Programme, Radio 4 occupied the Home Service's frequency and, in 1970, Radio 3 incorporated the Third Programme.

The whole shake-up of BBC Radio was, in part, a response to the threat of pirate radio stations such as Radio Caroline, which had started broadcasting from a ship off the Essex coast in 1964. In particular, the introduction of Radio 1 symbolised the BBC's (largely reluctant) acknowledgement that the craze for popular music wasn't just a flash in the pan, but was here to stay.

FRANK GILLARD (1908–1998)

It has been said that Frank Gillard was 'A West Country man by birth, upbringing, and conviction'. Despite that, however, he apparently had no nostalgia for the old ways when it came to BBC programmes. As the Director of Sound Broadcasting, one of the first things he did was to abolish *Children's Hour*, which was flagging in ratings, despite a public outcry backed up by a critical motion signed by sixty MPs.

A LITTLE 4 THOUGHT

As a war correspondent, one of Frank Gillard's notable reports came from an open-air church service in Normandy during the 1944 D-Day landings. Field Marshal Montgomery could be heard reading from the Bible, pausing when the fighter planes roared overhead.

KEEPING THE HOME FIRES BURNING

It is often said that the Home Service was the forerunner of Radio 4. While this is largely true, it is also an oversimplification. When it happened, the 1967 'switchover' was ostensibly between the Home Service and Radio 4, but in fact Radio 4 as we know it today has been shaped and influenced – and in some cases directly 'fed' programmes – by the National Programme, the Regional Programme, the Light Programme, the Third Programme and the Empire/Overseas Service.

In 1967, BBC Radio was not streamlined according to taste in the way it is today. Whereas we now think of Radio 2 as mainly popular music and chat, Radio 3 as classical music and drama, and Radio 4 as speech radio, programmes were often 'shared' between the stations. So a comedy series that went out on the Light Programme, or a drama that went out on the Third Programme, would be repeated on the Home Service, offering the material to a different audience. Radio 2, for example, still had comedy slots up until the 1990s.

Over time, as Radio 4 developed into speech radio, it inherited some of its programmes from the Light Programme/ Radio 2 (including *Woman's Hour* and *The Archers*), the Third Programme (such as drama), or one of the regional stations via the Home Service (such as *Gardeners' Question Time*).

Steve Arnold, of the *Radio Times* Archive, explains it in terms of a kind of aspirational hierarchy:

The channel structure was seen as a pyramid, with the Light at the base – accessible to all – the Home above that and there to encourage people to try out more... and the Third the pinnacle that all should aspire to.

The waters are also muddied by the fact that the switchover did not take place in one go. Indeed, the Home Service survived in some parts of the country for a considerable time after 1967, as the funding wasn't available to fully upgrade the local radio station network.

A LITTLE **4** THOUGHT

Radios 1, 2, 3 and 4 have been characterised as 'Pop, Cosy, Highbrow, and Everything Else'.

Until January 1983 people in what are now the BBC Radio Cornwall and BBC Radio Devon regions were still listening to what was in effect the last Regional Home Service.

THE FORMATIVE YEARS – 1970S, 1980S AND 1990S

If Radio 1 was the hip and groovy youngster in 1967, Radio 4 was a maiden aunt who had simply undergone a change of name. Indeed, many listeners would have noticed little if any change between Radio 4 and the Home Service. Spoken-word programmes, drama, serials, comedy, quizzes, discussion and mainstream classical music had become the substance of the Home Service schedule, and that was not about to change with the advent of Radio 4. Some of the programmes, such as *Desert Island Discs* and *Letter from America*, were so well established on the airwaves that they were set to celebrate their thousandth editions. In addition, during term time, Radio 4 still broadcast schools programming as part of its output – just as the Home Service had.

Nevertheless, change was afoot in the 1970s, and it was most noticeable in Radio 4's news and current affairs output. There was a move to dig deeper and look at stories from fresh angles. In 1970 a number of new programmes were introduced, among them *PM*, *Start the Week*, *Analysis* and the satirical *Week Ending*, while the investigative programme *File on 4* would become a feature of the airwaves by 1977.

Also in the 1970s programmes such as *You and Yours* started to champion (and arguably shape) a generation of consumers that had not previously been catered for. *Money Box* and *Does He Take Sugar?* both had listeners' interests at their core. Meanwhile in *Checkpoint*, Roger Cook was not content to represent the consumer from the studio but waded in, microphone in hand, to confront the corrupt and the crooked on behalf of the cheated.

This coincided with a drive to involve the Radio 4 listener more directly, and new technology was allowing for greater interactivity. *It's Your Line*, fronted by Robin Day, was Radio 4's first phone-in programme in 1970. *Feedback* was first aired in 1979, rounding off a decade in which the voice of the listener had become a feature of the airwaves.

Once a sedate maiden aunt, Radio 4 seemed to be getting more in tune with the spirit of the people. She was, however, still rather serious and perhaps a bit worthy. In the late 1970s and early 1980s, though, we started to glimpse her lighter side, particularly when it came to drama. Landmark serialisations such as *The Hitchhiker's Guide to the Galaxy* (1978), *The Lord of the Rings* (1981) and *Adrian Mole* (1982), and sitcoms such as Simon Brett's *After Henry* (1985–1989) started to demonstrate that Auntie did, after all, have a sense of humour.

A LITTLE **4** THOUGHT

You had to have a licence to listen to BBC Radio until February 1971.

In his autobiography *More Dangerous Ground*, Roger Cook recalled that he had been assaulted over sixteen times while making *Checkpoint*, suffering 'broken ribs, concussion, fractures, lacerations and bruises' in the process. But the incident that stayed with him was when a woman emptied a chamber pot over his head from an upstairs window. As it was radio, he had to continue giving a running commentary as it was happening.

The stars of *After Henry*, Prunella Scales and Joan Sanderson, both stayed with the show when it transferred to ITV in January 1988. As the radio version ran until March 1989, there was more than a year's overlap in which they were both appearing in both versions.

PRODUCER CHOICE

In the early 1990s the 'Producer Choice' initiative started to be discussed, and it soon became the hot topic in broadcast media, particularly at the BBC. Although the idea met with vocal opposition, it was introduced as policy in April 1993.

Producer Choice was the brainchild of Director General John Birt, whose idea was that introducing market forces and competition into the BBC would sharpen practices and encourage producers to keep their budgets under control.

BBC staff were divided into 'buyers' (producers) and 'sellers' (suppliers), with buyers being obliged to shop for resources – studio time, crews, archive material, etc. The 'choice' was that they could shop externally as well as internally. But whereas the buyers might have enjoyed increased choice, the sellers' jobs suddenly became dependent on doing enough 'business' with the buyers.

Producer Choice was hugely unpopular among BBC staff, and it was said, for example, that it had suddenly become cheaper to buy a CD on the high street than to borrow it from the BBC Library.

Although many Radio 4 programmes are now independently produced, the formal system of Producer Choice was dispensed with in 2006.

A LITTLE  THOUGHT

Gardeners' Question Time was one of the first programmes to be outsourced to an independent production company. When disagreements erupted between the panel and producers, the entire panel defected to Classic FM in 1994. The panel was replaced by a new team of experts, and the programme continues to this day.

In 1993 Radio 4's first gay and lesbian programme, a two-hour special called *Sunday Outing*, was presented by Matthew Parris and Bea Campbell.

MORE SCHEDULE CHANGES AND THE GREAT 'DUMBING DOWN' DEBATE

As the millennium approached, another schedule shake-up, this time under the leadership of Radio 4 controller James Boyle, proved highly controversial.

Among his sweeping changes, Boyle scrapped some programmes, introduced others, shuffled some around, and extended or reduced others in length. Those changes affected established Radio 4 institutions, including *The Archers*, *Today*, *Woman's Hour*, *Yesterday in Parliament* and *Kaleidoscope*. Among the programmes he introduced were *Home Truths*, the Saturday morning programme fronted by former Radio 1 DJ John Peel, and the arts programme *Front Row*, although this was at the expense of *Kaleidoscope*.

Many of Boyle's innovations were met with disgust from listeners and open dissent from presenters and staff. For a while it looked as though they were right, and his changes had a detrimental effect on Radio 4's ratings. In 1999, figures revealed that the station had haemorrhaged 600,000 listeners, and that the total radio-listening public had fallen to an all-time low of under eight million.

Ultimately, however, listeners and staff settled back into a routine and, shock horror, even found themselves enjoying *Home Truths* and *Front Row*.

RADIO 4 NOW

Much more than just the programmes, the bits in between are what make Radio 4 familiar to its listeners. This chapter is about all those bits – the *Shipping Forecast* and the pips, bongs and music that make this aural landscape 'home'.

THE *SHIPPING FORECAST*

It has been pointed out that a large proportion of the *Shipping Forecast*'s regular listeners are land-based, rarely if ever venturing out to sea. That fact is testament to the addictive nature of this fixture of Radio 4, because there is something thrilling and transporting about hearing the news out at sea, particularly when you are warm and safe at home – it is something which brings home to us the fact that we are an island nation and which, in the dead of night or very early morning, reminds us that life is going on out there on the open seas.

The *Shipping Forecast* has been broadcast on Radio 4 since it transferred to long wave in 1978. The Met Office issues four forecasts a day, at 11 p.m., 5 a.m., 11 a.m. and 5 p.m., each one covering a twenty-four-hour period starting one hour after issue. Radio 4 FM and LW broadcasts these at 12.48 a.m. and 5.20 a.m., and following the midday news and at 5.54 p.m. on long wave only (except the 5.54 p.m. is broadcast on both wavelengths at weekends).

The introductory forecast contains information about gale warnings and a general synopsis, while the specific sea-area forecasts contain information about wind direction, weather and visibility.

A LITTLE 4 THOUGHT

The shipping forecast was developed by Robert FitzRoy after a great storm of 1859 wrecked a steam clipper off Anglesey with the loss of 450 lives. FitzRoy's warning service used telegraph communication, and was introduced in 1861.

Nothing interrupts the *Shipping Forecast*. Cricket fans can tell you about the times during the 2011 Ashes when it interrupted three of England's victorious wicket-taking moments.

THE SHIPPING FORECAST MAP

There are thirty-one areas on the shipping forecast map. The overall area of the map extends south as far as the west coast of Spain (Trafalgar), to the north as far as south-east Iceland, as far east as Denmark (German Bight) and as far west as off the west coast of Ireland (Shannon).

Starting with Viking, at two o'clock, they are named in a roughly clockwise direction. Here are the origins of some of their names:

Viking, Forties, Dogger, Fisher, Sole and Bailey are named after sandbanks.

Cromarty, Forth, Tyne, Humber, Thames and Shannon are named after estuaries.

Wight, Lundy, Fair Isle, Faeroes, Portland, Hebrides, South-east Iceland and North and South Utsire are named after islands.

The German Bight is an indentation on the northern European shoreline.

Dover and Plymouth are named after the English town and city respectively.

Rockall and Fastnet are both named after islets.

Malin is named after Malin Head, the northernmost point of Ireland.

Biscay is named after the Bay of Biscay, and Trafalgar after Cape Trafalgar.

Irish Sea is named, not surprisingly, after the Irish Sea.

FitzRoy (which used to be Finisterre) is named after Vice-Admiral Robert FitzRoy, who devised the original shipping forecast.

THE THIRTY-ONE AREAS IN THE ORDER IN WHICH THEY ARE ANNOUNCED

Viking, North Utsire, South Utsire, Forties, Cromarty, Forth, Tyne, Dogger, Fisher, German Bight, Humber, Thames, Dover, Wight, Portland, Plymouth, Biscay, Trafalgar, FitzRoy, Sole, Lundy, Fastnet, Irish Sea, Shannon, Rockall, Malin, Hebrides, Bailey, Fair Isle, Faeroes, South-east Iceland.

A LITTLE 4 THOUGHT

The forecast for Trafalgar is broadcast only in the 12.48 a.m. forecast unless there are gale warnings.

The term used in the shipping forecast is 'hurricane force'; the term 'hurricane' on its own means a true tropical cyclone, not experienced in British waters.

As well as a pioneering meteorologist, Robert FitzRoy (1805–1865), after whom the shipping area is named, was captain of HMS *Beagle* during Charles Darwin's famous voyage.

The shipping forecast was suspended in all its forms during both world wars.

The most familiar voice of the *Shipping Forecast* was Peter Jefferson, who read it for forty years between 1969 and 2009. Other readers include Charlotte Green, Alice Arnold, Kathy Clugston and Zeb Soanes.

In 2009, when Peter Jefferson fluffed his lines, he was heard muttering 'f***' over the pips. He retired shortly afterwards, although rumours persisted that he had been sacked.

When, at 5.20 a.m. on 30 May 2014, Radio 4 accidentally missed the *Shipping Forecast* and played the World Service output instead, one listener tweeted: 'Isn't that the sign of impending nuclear Armageddon?'

CELEBRITY VOICES

Over the years the *Shipping Forecast* has from time to time been read by celebrity readers, including:

John Prescott, who read it for Red Nose Day 2011. This came about after he tweeted that he was doing an interview for *The World Tonight* and might as well stay on to do the *Shipping*

Forecast. Announcer Alice Arnold spotted it and tweeted back that he was welcome to do it 'so I could go home early'.

In 2013 Alan Bennett was invited to read it by Michael Palin when he guest-edited *Today*. His reading was broadcast in December, although the forecast was from a particularly stormy day in October.

THE *SHIPPING FORECAST* IN ART

It has been pointed out that the *Shipping Forecast* is read like a poetry recital. Certainly, over the years its mesmerising tones have inspired artists, poets and musicians – and part of the *Shipping Forecast* was recited during Danny Boyle's opening ceremony of the 2012 London Olympic Games.

Here are just a few examples of *Shipping Forecast*-inspired creativity:

In December 1993 it was read by announcer Laurie Macmillan on both radio and BBC2 as part of *Arena*'s Radio Night.

'The Shipping Forecast Rap' is a song by Snoop Doggy Dogger.

Composer Cecilia McDowall was commissioned to set the *Shipping Forecast* to music for the Portsmouth Festival Choir in 2011.

'Glanmore Sonnets VII', a poem by Seamus Heaney, opens with the words: 'Dogger, Rockall, Malin, Irish Sea…'

'This is a Low', a song by Blur, contains part of the *Shipping Forecast*, as does 'In Limbo' by Radiohead.

THE SOUNDS OF RADIO 4

Whether we're aware of them or not, the sounds of Radio 4 – the music, pips and bongs – are just as familiar to listeners as the dulcet tones of John Humphrys, Martha Kearney, Jenni Murray and Eddie Mair.

THE RADIO 4 THEME

Although it no longer graces the airwaves, the Radio 4 Theme was such an integral part of Radio 4 it deserves a mention. Composed by Fritz Spiegl and arranged by Manfred Arlan, the medley of traditional British airs was played every morning between 1978 and 2006, marking the handover between the World Service and Radio 4.

In 2006, controller Mark Damazer's decision to cancel the Radio 4 Theme to make way for a news briefing caused consternation. When the axe fell it's probably fair to say there was rejoicing in some quarters, indignation in others.

For the sake of nostalgia, here is a rundown of the tunes, which take the listener on a jaunt around the British Isles:

'Early One Morning'

'Rule, Britannia'

'Danny Boy'

'What Shall We Do with the Drunken Sailor?'

'Greensleeves'

'Men of Harlech'

'Scotland the Brave'

'Rule Britannia' combined with the 'Trumpet Voluntary'

A LITTLE 4 THOUGHT

In 2006, Glenda Jackson's signature was one of those on a motion tabled in the House of Commons that read: 'This House considers that the UK theme on BBC Radio 4 is extremely irritating.'

'SAILING BY'

'Sailing By' is a slow waltz which is played before the 12.48 a.m. *Shipping Forecast*. It was composed in 1963 by Ronald Binge, and has been used for the forecast since 1967 – almost without interruption. The exception to this was in 1993, when it was briefly taken off air after (misguided) rumours circulated that the royalties were the equivalent of the salary of a member of staff.

PIPS, BONGS AND TIMEKEEPING

Timing is sacrosanct on Radio 4. At the start of each hour, the Greenwich Time Signal, known as 'the pips', is broadcast. The exceptions to this are midnight and 6 p.m., when the chimes of Big Ben ('the bongs') are played.

The pips were introduced in 1924 and were originally supplied by the Royal Greenwich Observatory after an agreement between John Reith and the Astronomer Royal. Since 1990, the pips have been generated by the BBC from the lower ground floor of Broadcasting House.

Usually, five short pips are followed by a long pip, which sounds on the hour – the last pip has been elongated since the 1980s to indicate the precise hour. It is required because every now and again a 'leap second' is indicated by an additional seventh pip.

A LITTLE 4 THOUGHT

Running over at the end of a programme is known as 'crashing the pips'. The presenters of the *Today* programme are particularly famous (or perhaps infamous) for doing this.

Each of the short pips lasts 100 milliseconds, while the elongated pip is 500 milliseconds long.

In 2011 *The News Quiz* featured a special pantomime in which the pips went missing. As the BBC never permits them to be broadcast except as a time signal, only individual pips were played.

66 For some extraordinary reason...
I said it was twenty-eight minutes past eight...
It's actually twenty-two minutes past seven.
Please forgive me. 99

JACK DE MANIO, THE *TODAY* PRESENTER FAMOUS FOR NOT BEING ABLE TO TELL THE TIME

LONG WAVE

The term 'long wave' dates back to the early twentieth century, when the radio spectrum was considered to consist of long, medium and short wavelengths.

Although it is old technology, long wave still has its advantages over other frequencies. It is not the clearest, but on the other hand it can reach the places that other frequencies cannot – so a submarine can receive long wave, for example, but not FM. In addition, the range of the signal is such that ships can pick up the *Shipping Forecast* on long wave.

The BBC has been using FM frequencies since 1955, although for many years after that medium-wave broadcasting was predominant. Radio 4 began transmission on long wave (200 KHz) in 1978 and, apart from a two-degree shift to 198 KHz in 1988, has remained the same ever since.

Until 1990, Radio 4's FM frequencies carried educational programming (Open University, schools and adult education) at various times of the day, in much the way that long wave now carries 'niche' programming. When Radio 5 was launched in 1990, it started to carry the BBC's educational content. That, coupled with the extension of FM coverage throughout the UK by 1991, enabled the FM service to become the mainstream Radio 4 service.

These days the vast majority of Radio 4 listeners rely on FM or digital radio rather than long wave, which is used to carry a few programmes that are considered too niche for mainstream Radio 4.

The best-known programme broadcast on long wave is *Test Match Special*, which would otherwise dominate huge swathes of the FM schedule. In addition, *Yesterday in Parliament* airs at 8.30 a.m. in the weeks when Parliament is sitting, cutting out the last 30 minutes of *Today*, while the *Daily Service* is carried on long wave every weekday at 9.45 a.m., when FM and digital listeners are tuned in to *Book of the Week*.

In addition, two programmes – the *Midday News* and *PM* – are kept slightly shorter on long wave in order to accommodate the *Shipping Forecast*.

A LITTLE 4 THOUGHT

The hertz is named after Heinrich Rudolf Hertz, who conclusively proved the existence of electromagnetic waves.

WAVE GOODBYE TO LONG WAVE?

In 1992, the BBC announced plans to rededicate the Radio 4 long-wave frequency as a rolling twenty-four-hour news service, and confine Radio 4 to FM. It sparked a fierce 'Middle-England' protest, which resulted in the BBC agreeing that the change would not be introduced until they were certain that listeners' needs throughout the UK would be met. In the end, it was decided to rededicate Radio 5 as the continuous news and sport network Radio 5 Live.

It was, however, to be only a temporary reprieve for Radio 4 LW. In 2011, BBC Director General Mark Thompson announced that there would be no further investment in long wave. It was explained that the Droitwich transmitter is reliant on a pair of ancient metre-high specially crafted glass valves that last anywhere between one and ten years, and that there were fewer than ten of these left in the world. The BBC had bought up the entire global supply and decided not to go to the expense of making new ones. It was also explained that the existing valves were not only costly, but also almost impossible to replicate, meaning that the slightest flaw could cause a catastrophic failure of the other parts of the transmitter.

As modern mariners tend to use other technology to get shipping information, and the number of homes reliant on long wave is diminishing all the time, the decision had been taken not to go to the expense of having new valves manufactured.

All of this means that when one of the last two valves blows, Radio 4 LW will go suddenly and permanently off air. It was not executed in 1992, but it is ailing and there is a 'Do not resuscitate' sign hanging over it.

A LITTLE 4 THOUGHT

The two Droitwich long-wave transmission masts are 213 metres (700 feet) high. At over three times their height (646 metres or 2,120 feet) the Warsaw Radio Mast was the world's tallest structure – until it collapsed in 1991.

From time to time, in addition to its regular schedule, Radio 4 LW broadcasts special events, such as Pope Benedict XVI's 2010 visit to Britain, which was covered by Ed Stourton.

The long-wave signal is part of the Royal Navy's system of 'Last Resort Letters'. It is said that, in the event of a suspected catastrophic attack on Britain, submarine commanders are briefed to check for a signal from Radio 4 LW to establish whether or not organised society in Great Britain has been annihilated. Let's hope somebody tells them when the final transmitter valves blow…

Test Match Special takes precedence over on-the-hour news bulletins on Radio 4 LW, but (as we have seen) much to the annoyance of cricket fans, gives way to the *Shipping Forecast*.

BROADCASTING HOUSE

When it was opened in 1932, the state-of-the-art Art Deco building Broadcasting House was the first of its kind in the UK, purpose-built for broadcasting.

It was traditionally the home of BBC Radio but, with the closure of BBC Television Centre in March 2013 and the move of much of the BBC's operations to Salford, Broadcasting House has been redeveloped, restored and extended to become the BBC's London headquarters. The building is home to BBC News, along with other radio, television and online services. At its heart is the biggest live newsroom in Europe.

A LITTLE **4** THOUGHT

The iconic statue outside Broadcasting House is of Ariel and Prospero by sculptor Eric Gill. It's said that there was such an outcry about Ariel's nudity that John Reith decreed that Ariel's member should be reduced in size.

The John Peel Wing is part of New Broadcasting House, in memory of the late DJ.

RADIO 4 IN THE DIGITAL AGE

A TIMELINE

1995 The BBC begins the world's first digital audio broadcasting (DAB) transmissions.

1996 The Broadcasting Act sets out plans for the launch of digital broadcasting.

2001 The first portable digital radios go on sale.

2002 The BBC launches five new digital radio networks – 1Xtra, 5 Live Sports Extra, 6 Music, Radio 7 and the Asian Network.

2007 BBC iPlayer is launched.

The Digital Radio Working Group (DRWG) is established.

Start of the region-by-region analogue switch-off process for television.

2010 The government launches its Digital Radio Action Plan, which emphasises that digital radio switchover should begin only when the market is ready and should be consumer-led. The aspirational target date is 2015, providing the following criteria have been met:

50 per cent of all radio listening must be via digital platforms.

National DAB coverage must be comparable to FM, and local DAB must reach 90 per cent of the population and all major roads.

2011   Radio 7 is relaunched as Radio 4 Extra.

2012   Ofcom publishes a report on the availability and take-up of digital radio services. It finds that:

25.9 per cent of new cars are now fitted with DAB as standard.

Among those who do not yet have access to a DAB radio at home, 19 per cent claim that they are 'likely', 'very likely' or 'certain' to buy a set in the next twelve months.

49 per cent of respondents without a DAB radio at home said they were 'not likely' to buy one within the next year.

2013   Communications Minister Ed Vaizey announces that the radio industry will have to wait for digital switchover, as digital take-up had been slower than expected and accounts for just over a third of all radio listening.

A LITTLE 4 THOUGHT

In 2002, Paul Merton launched Radio 7, later to become Radio 4 Extra. Its output remains essentially unchanged, although, as you might expect, Radio 4 Extra has a higher Radio 4 content.

Journalist Ben Hammersley invented the word 'podcast' when he was writing an article for *The Guardian* about the new phenomenon of automatically downloading audio programmes.

TERMS EXPLAINED FOR THE TECHNOLOGICALLY CHALLENGED

For those who have never heard 'stream' used as a verb, it might sound strange that many people access BBC programmes via 'streaming'. Here are a few helpful definitions:

Download: Transfer data from one computer system to another, usually from a web server, via the Internet.

Stream: Access audio or visual material over the Internet as a continuous, real-time stream of data.

BBC iPlayer: A software application created and managed by the BBC to provide Internet television and radio services. Programmes watched or listened to using iPlayer are streamed.

In other words, if you download a radio podcast, you are storing it on a hard drive or portable media device (such as an iPod). It will be available for you to listen to again whether or not you are connected to the Internet. If you stream a radio programme over iPlayer, you have to be connected to the Internet to hear it, and it will only be available for a limited time.

A LITTLE 4 THOUGHT

Digital broadcasts lag slightly behind those on FM because the processes used in sending information are different. Some (non-BBC) radio stations delay their analogue signal to make any time delay less noticeable.

Figures for the first quarter of 2014 showed that the average radio listener tunes into 21.5 hours of radio per week.

The Royal Charter is the constitutional basis for the BBC, and must be regularly renewed. The charter granted in 2006 runs until 31 December 2016.

The Caribbean accent you hear from time to time on Radio 4 continuity announcements belongs to Jamaican-born Neil Nunes. His appointment in 2006 caused predictable controversy, with some listeners objecting to a 'foreign' accent, while others dismissed this 'Little Englander' attitude.

Portrait of the Presenter As a Listener
LIBBY PURVES
Presenter, *Midweek*

My first memory of the home service is... as a child, having lived abroad a lot, loving visits to the UK because I could hear *Just a Minute* and *The Goon Show* and the rest... I sent off for a kit to make a little pocket transistor radio so I could have it privately to listen to in my bedroom or my tent on the lawn.

When I'm not working I'm listening to... a lot of Radio 4, until something comes on which drives me nuts. I like to be surprised by documentaries, plays, etc., and am a closet Eddie Mair fan on *PM*.

Radio 4 matters because... it is the only source of quality, crafted, intelligent speech radio, which is the nimblest and most versatile and vivid of all media ever invented, combining eloquence and sound.

66 *The best thing about Radio 4 is the randomness of subjects! It's amazing what is covered in a day's listening... so much better than school ever was!* 99

SAZ WILTSHIRE, DESIGNER

AND NOW FOR THE NEWS

A BRIEF HISTORY OF BBC RADIO NEWS

In the beginning, the news itself was news. The BBC's first ever on-air news bulletin was read at 6 p.m. on 15 November 1922 by Director of Programmes Arthur Burrows.

The following evening's bulletin contained the news that: 'For the first time in history, news was broadcast in England last night by the British Broadcasting Company.'

However, and perhaps surprisingly, the dissemination of news was not really on the agenda in the early days. For one thing, news-gathering was considered too costly, so the BBC confined its activities to simply broadcasting news gathered from other sources. Each bulletin opened with a copyright announcement crediting Reuters, the Press Association, Exchange Telegraph and Central News. For another thing, the paparazzi were extremely jittery about the competition that broadcasting represented and were concerned to keep their market share. So it was agreed that no news bulletins would be broadcast before 7 p.m. each day, with General Manager John Reith commenting: 'I do not think there is much demand for an earlier bulletin.'

But although the BBC deferred to the print media, the listening public was voting through the radio dial and, the day after the 1922 general election, *The Times* noted the phenomenon of 'listening-in parties' when thousands of people were able to 'sit comfortably at home and learn by wireless the news'.

The balance shifted decisively during the 1926 General Strike. On Friday 30 April, John Reith interrupted a late-night dance-music programme to announce that a strike had been called for the following Monday. During the strike the printing presses were silent due to the printworkers' involvement in the strike. Reith seized the opportunity and negotiated with the government to lift the ban on broadcast news. Soon five radio news bulletins were being transmitted daily, and news was firmly on the BBC's agenda. In 1927 and 1928, the amount of news in BBC Radio's output doubled.

But while the quantity of news might have increased, Reith was still frustrated by restrictions on the content. No editorial opinion was permitted although, from 1928, the corporation was able to broadcast on 'matters of political, industrial or religious controversy'.

During the 1930s, the relationship with the news agencies became weaker as new technology enabled the BBC to work more autonomously. Reith was very keen to keep BBC Radio News distinct from Fleet Street. There would be no sensationalism at the BBC, parliamentary news was given greater prominence than elsewhere, and newsreaders were strictly anonymous (although a list of names was leaked by the *Daily Express* in 1932).

A LITTLE **4** THOUGHT

Public information bulletins – such as Christmas posting dates and traffic bulletins – originally formed part of the news, until there were so many that they had to be hived off into a separate slot.

On 18 April 1930, during what should have been a 6.30 p.m. news bulletin, a BBC presenter announced 'Good evening. Today is Good Friday. There is no news.' Piano music was then played for a couple of minutes, before normal scheduling resumed.

Vernon Bartlett is often considered to have been the BBC's first foreign correspondent. His contract was not renewed after his coverage of Hitler's decision to leave the League of Nations in 1933 was deemed 'not beastly enough'.

In 1933 the national news was read by a woman. It was an experiment that did not last long, and any momentous news was read by John Reith himself. In January 1936, for example, it was his voice which announced the death of King George V.

WARTIME

From the outbreak of war in 1939, there was tension between the BBC and the government over how much freedom should be allowed to BBC Radio News, and it took time to establish an effective way of working between the BBC and the new Ministry of Information.

There was a nervousness about the enemy listening in to radio broadcasts. Over the years the number of daily bulletins had risen to ten, but in September 1939 it was reduced to six. At the government's insistence the news was kept vague. For example, 'heavy bombing on the south coast' was often as specific as a report would be, to downplay the impact of any attacks and prevent the Luftwaffe from knowing which of its sorties had found their targets. Weather forecasts were dispensed with altogether, for fear of imparting useful information to enemy planes.

Despite all the restrictions, the Home Service news was a lifeline of information to households all around the country. The *Nine O'Clock News* bulletin provided a focus for the nation, and listening audiences regularly numbered sixteen million – half the adult population.

In 1940 newsreaders started to be named, to enable listeners to be sure that they were indeed listening to the authentic BBC news. It was pointed out, however, that all the male newsreaders, with their cut-glass accents, sounded rather similar, and that it wouldn't be too hard to impersonate any of them. It led to the appointment of Wilfred Pickles with his broad Yorkshire accent. He made his debut in 1941 and became an instant hit, particularly north of the Watford Gap.

During the war the Overseas Service (later the World Service) and the European Service played a particularly important role in spreading radio news around the globe and by the end of 1940 the BBC was broadcasting in thirty-four languages. The explosion in overseas broadcasting dramatically changed the technology across all the BBC's services, particularly when it came to the news.

Reporters trained in map reading and aircraft identification started sending eyewitness accounts from the front line. To do this they had the latest technology, the new 'Midget' recorder, which had been developed by BBC engineers. A kind of wind-up gramophone, it recorded a maximum of 2 minutes' worth of material on discs and weighed about thirty pounds – yet it gave BBC correspondents a new freedom.

A LITTLE 4 THOUGHT

During World War Two the government forbade all on-air mention of the names of military regiments and the whereabouts of members of the Royal Family.

When Broadcasting House was bombed in 1940, it was during a newscast read by Bruce Belfrage. Despite being covered in plaster and soot, Belfrage carried on as though nothing had happened, and the only interruption for listeners at home was a dull thud. Tragically, however, seven people lost their lives in the blast.

WAR REPORT

D-Day marked a new direction in radio news broadcasting, with the introduction of *War Report* – a half-hour programme designed to bring the 'latest and fullest picture of the war'. It was innovative in that correspondents' voices were heard on the radio for the first time, as opposed to the announcer or newsreader reading what had been reported on the ground. *War Report* brought listeners the sounds and drama of the D-Day beaches, the advance through Normandy, the liberation of Paris, Arnhem, and finally the German surrender in May 1945.

A LITTLE 4 THOUGHT

Richard Dimbleby was a *War Report* correspondent, as was Frank Gillard. It was Gillard who, as Managing Director of BBC Radio in 1967, was instrumental in the introduction of Radios 1, 2, 3 and 4.

> One particularly shocking *War Report* came from Richard Dimbleby in April 1945, in which he recounted the horror of Belsen. At first the BBC refused to broadcast it, but capitulated when Dimbleby threatened to resign.

POST-WAR NEWS

During the 1950s television became a much bigger part of everyday life for people. Television news started in the 1950s, and commercial television was introduced in 1955. During the 1956 Suez Crisis it was to their TVs rather than their radios that people turned for updates on the situation.

As late as 1958, however, all news-gathering and many of the editorial functions – for both television and radio – were still the remit of BBC Radio. The result was rather stilted television news, whereby viewers would see a BBC newsreader who handed over to a radio newsreader, who would read the news over a series of still images such as maps and photographs.

When he was Head of News and Current Affairs, Hugh Carleton Greene made BBC Television News autonomous, and for nearly thirty years after that the two news services operated more or less independently of each other.

THE NEWS ON TAP

In 1991 an unexpected development changed the face of BBC News – and it started with the midnight news on Radio 4.

On 16 January, the Allied forces started bombing Iraq in response to the invasion of Kuwait. The decision was made to keep broadcasting the news, extending a half-hour bulletin to 4 hours. By the next morning arrangements were in place to move Radio 4's usual output to long wave and keep transmitting news about the Gulf War on FM.

For the next six weeks 'Scud FM', as it was nicknamed, kept broadcasting, paving the way for twenty-four-hour news on both radio and television. BBC Radio 5 Live was launched in 1994, and BBC News 24 in 1997.

JOINED-UP THINKING

Whereas Carleton Greene had driven a wedge between television and radio news in the late 1950s, in the late 1980s John Birt revived the practice of correspondents working across both media. As the culmination of his vision for 'bi-media' journalism, in 1997 BBC Radio News journalists left Broadcasting House to join their television colleagues in a purpose-built extension to BBC Television Centre in Shepherd's Bush.

There were well-documented frustrations after the move. Whereas at one time you might have found a radio news reporter working alongside a television reporter to produce the same report for different media, the grumbles around the new system centred on the tussle for resources, with the same reporter now potentially having to meet several different deadlines. In the era of twenty-four-hour news the pressure was more than doubled.

Just three years after the radio journalists had completed the move to Television Centre, an announcement was made that BBC Radio News journalists would ultimately move back to Broadcasting House – this time taking their television colleagues with them. The BBC insisted that licence-payers' money would not be involved.

John Birt's vision came to fruition, but not completely. For one thing, unforeseen technological advances meant that bi-media journalism had to make way for 'tri-media journalism' across television, radio and the Internet.

These days news-gathering is still centrally managed across all three media, although the news output is produced by editorial staff in separate television and radio departments. With the closure of Television Centre in 2013, the move to the refurbished and extended Broadcasting House was completed.

A LITTLE 4 THOUGHT

BBC News is the world's largest broadcast news organisation, each day generating about 120 hours of radio and television news output, plus online coverage.

In 2013, in a 30-second news item, the intrepid newsreader and announcer Neil Sleat was confronted by a Hawaiian name containing thirty-five letters: Keihanaikukauakahihuliheekahaunaele. He pronounced it correctly – twice.

NEWS ROUND THE CLOCK

A typical weekday Radio 4 news schedule looks as follows:

Midnight	*Midnight News*
5.30 a.m.	*News Briefing*
6 a.m.	*Today*
7 a.m.	Hourly news bulletin
8 a.m.	Hourly news bulletin
9 a.m.	Hourly news bulletin
10 a.m.	Hourly news bulletin
11 a.m.	Hourly news bulletin
Midday	Hourly news bulletin
1 p.m.	*World at One (WATO)*

2 p.m.	Hourly news bulletin
3 p.m.	Hourly news bulletin
4 p.m.	Hourly news bulletin
5 p.m.	*PM*
6 p.m.	*Six O'Clock News*
7 p.m.	Hourly news bulletin
8 p.m.	Hourly news bulletin
8–8.30 p.m.	A business or economics strand such as *File on 4*, *The Bottom Line*, *In Business*
9 p.m.	Hourly news bulletin
10 p.m.	*The World Tonight*
11 p.m.	Hourly news bulletin

WEEKEND NEWS SCHEDULE VARIATIONS:

The 5.30 a.m. *News Briefing* and hourly bulletins are a feature of Saturday and Sunday just like any other day.

On weekend mornings, *News and Papers* takes a look at the news headlines and how they have been reported in the papers.

On Saturday a shorter version of *Today* is broadcast between 7 a.m. and 9 a.m. At 1 p.m. *WATO* is replaced by a shorter news bulletin followed by *Any Questions?* and *Any Answers? PM's* listener-led sister programme, *iPM*, is broadcast at 5.45 a.m. and again at 5.30 p.m., following *Saturday PM*.

On Sunday, the news magazine programme *Broadcasting House* airs between 9 a.m. and 10 a.m. *WATO's* sister programme *The World This Weekend*, presented by Shaun Ley, is broadcast between 1 p.m. and 1.30 p.m. Tuesday's *File on 4* is repeated at 5 p.m. *What the Papers Say* is broadcast between 10.45 p.m. and 11 p.m.

WORLD AT ONE (WATO)

PROGRAMME STATS

Running since: 1965

Current presenters: Martha Kearney (@Marthakearney), Shaun Ley (@BBCShaunLey)

Some past presenters and producers: Jenny Abramsky, George Alagiah, Ben Bradshaw, Roger Cook, Jonathan Dimbleby, Pallab Ghosh, David Jessel, Kirsty Lang, Sue MacGregor, Nick Ross, Kirsty Wark, Sian Williams

Listening figures: 3.1 million (weekly figures from RAJAR for the first quarter of 2014)

Description: 45 minutes of news, analysis and comment.

Related programmes: *The World Tonight, The World This Weekend*

Website: www.bbc.co.uk/programmes/b006qptc

Twitter: @BBCWorldatOne

The introduction of *World at One* on the Home Service in 1965 was not uncontroversial, sparking what was arguably the first of many 'dumbing down' debates surrounding the Home Service and Radio 4.

It came about because Head of BBC News Donald Edwards wanted to replace 'long, stilted' news bulletins with a fresh approach, so he shortened the *One O'Clock News* and introduced *WATO* as a 'lively news and discussion magazine'.

It provoked outrage, and Edwards later said that some of the older radio newsmen never forgave him. But he forged ahead anyway, and installed the fast-talking William Hardcastle, a former editor of the *Daily Mail*, as *WATO*'s first presenter.

The new thing about *WATO* was that it was a mixture of news and current affairs, so it started to blur the distinction between news and comment – something the self-styled moral crusader Mary Whitehouse was not slow in picking up. In 1967 she attacked *WATO* for secularism and extreme views, in response to comments made on the programme by scriptwriter Johnny Speight. It was part of an ongoing feud between Whitehouse and Speight, whose television comedy *Til Death Us Do Part* had been one of the first programmes to use the word 'bloody'. Speight's comments had indeed been extreme, and with Quintin Hogg (later Lord Hailsham) as her representative, Whitehouse sued the BBC, who settled for £300.

Although its length has been chopped and changed over the years, *WATO*'s slot in the schedule is, by virtue of its name, set in stone. With over three million weekly listeners it is now comfortably installed as one of Radio 4's flagship news and current affairs programmes.

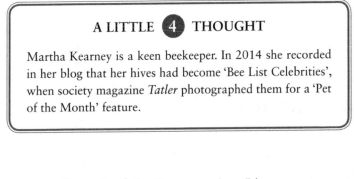

A LITTLE **4** THOUGHT

Martha Kearney is a keen beekeeper. In 2014 she recorded in her blog that her hives had become 'Bee List Celebrities', when society magazine *Tatler* photographed them for a 'Pet of the Month' feature.

Portrait of the Presenter As a Listener
SHAUN LEY
Presenter, *World at One* and *The World This Weekend*

My first memory of Radio 4... is being in one of the radio drama studios at Pebble Mill in Birmingham, in September 1981. I'd been cast in a drama called *The Hessian*. It was produced by a youthful and enthusiastic Vanessa Whitburn, later to become the long-serving editor of *The Archers*, and there were one or two Ambridge regulars among the cast. Derek Jacobi was the star turn, but I think my father was more impressed by a familiar Home Service voice from his childhood, Noel Johnson, who once played Dick Barton – Special Agent. For me, at twelve, the big fascination was the work of the Studio Manager, creating the sound effects, including bobbing something into a washing bowl to simulate my fishing trip in rural eighteenth-century Connecticut.

When I'm not working, I'm listening to... Radio 4 Extra, a cornucopia of past treasures, and a reminder of just how rich is BBC Radio's legacy. It's also a standing rebuke to those in the past who neglected our broadcast heritage, and a testament to the commitment of the listeners who recorded programmes at home. Without them, many great moments of radio would have been lost for good.

Radio matters because... there's more to life than what's happening right now. There are endless ways in which one can sample the present, especially in such an interconnected age. What matters is context, and Radio 4 creates a space in which the path that has shaped the present can be explored, and the horizon glimpsed of what may lie ahead. Knowing that's being shared at the same moment with millions of others is humbling.

PM

PROGRAMME STATS

Running since: 1970

Current presenters: Eddie Mair (@eddiemair), Carolyn Quinn (@carolynquinncq)

Past presenters: Joan Bakewell, Derek Cooper, William Hardcastle, Steve Race, Valerie Singleton, Hugh Sykes

Listening figures: 4 million (weekly figures from RAJAR for the first quarter of 2014)

Description: Coverage and analysis of the day's news.

Related programmes: *Saturday PM, iPM*

Website: www.bbc.co.uk/programmes/b006qskw

Twitter: @BBCPM

PM was introduced to the schedule just three years after the inception of Radio 4, with presenters William Hardcastle and Derek Cooper promising a programme that 'sums up the day, and your evening starts here'.

Over the years, *PM* has developed a reputation for being able to respond quickly to breaking news. And that's just as well, given that the 5–6 p.m. slot seems to be prone to big stories: revelations about Anthony Blunt; the attempt on Pope John Paul II's life; the explosion of the space shuttle *Challenger*; the Church of England's vote for women priests; John Major's resignation – all stories which broke while *PM* was on air.

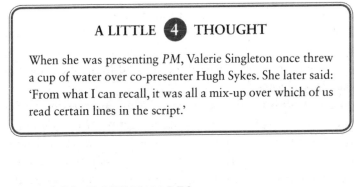

A LITTLE 4 THOUGHT

When she was presenting *PM*, Valerie Singleton once threw a cup of water over co-presenter Hugh Sykes. She later said: 'From what I can recall, it was all a mix-up over which of us read certain lines in the script.'

UPSHARES, DOWNSHARES

In response to the economic downturn in 2008, *PM* launched a daily business slot and asked listeners to name it. When someone came up with the title 'Upshares, Downshares', the producers used the original theme tune from the television drama *Upstairs,*

Downstairs, composed by Sandy Faris. Little could they have guessed what would happen next...

First, one listener sent in their own version of the theme tune, then another, until it snowballed and the *PM* office was receiving CDs, tapes and electronic versions on a daily basis. They included a calypso version, a dance version, a rock version, a *Dr Who* one, church bells, a rendition by a school recorder club and many, many more.

Even the distinguished composer John Tavener sent in his own composition ('in the style of Russ Conway') and the BBC Philharmonic Orchestra played a newly orchestrated version of the theme.

(Nearly) all of the variations were released on a CD sold in aid of Children in Need 2010.

PESTON VS MAIR

Nobody quite knows whether the famous feud between the two journalists is real or acted up for the listeners.

It began live on air during *PM* in January 2011, when Peston chastised Mair for ignoring his scoop about bankers' bonuses. In a programme later that year, he accused Mair of casting him 'into the wilderness'.

In 2013, with maximum sarcasm, Mair interviewed Peston about his new programme *Robert Peston Goes Shopping*. After Peston talked about the programme at some length, Mair, in his soft Scottish brogue, seamlessly wove a series of scathing insults into the interview. When Peston reminded Mair that he had described it as 'appointment television', Mair retorted that he had called it 'disappointment television'. The feud continues...

THINGS YOU (PROBABLY) NEVER KNEW ABOUT EDDIE MAIR

His broadcasting career is said to have started when he used the public address system in the school playground.

In 2013 he stood in on BBC1's *Andrew Marr Show* when Marr was recovering from a stroke. On one occasion he gave Boris Johnson, the Mayor of London, a thorough, if softly spoken, drubbing. *The Guardian* later described it as 'a bicycle crash: spokes all over the road, wheels mangled and a reputation badly dented'.

He writes a column in the *Radio Times*. When in 2014 the editor asked him to share his memories of Lord Patten, the outgoing chairman of the BBC Trust, what appeared in print was a blank hole.

THE WORLD TONIGHT

PROGRAMME STATS

Running since: 1968

Current presenter: Ritula Shah (@ritula)

Past presenter: Robin Lustig

Listening figures: 1.8 million (weekly figures from RAJAR for the first quarter of 2014)

Description: In-depth reporting and analysis from a global perspective.

Website: www.bbc.co.uk/programmes/b006qtl3

Twitter: @BBCWorldTonight

Portrait of the Presenter As a Listener
RITULA SHAH

Former Producer of *Today* and Presenter of *The World Tonight*
and *Saturday PM*

My first memory of Radio 4 is... *Listen With Mother*. My mum was always busy but she had the radio on all the time and *Listen With Mother* was the highlight of my day. I would sit on a kitchen stool and listen while Mum washed up after lunch. I loved the songs. Once I began school, Mum would wake me up and put *Today* on. I started young!

BROADCASTING HOUSE

PROGRAMME STATS

Running since: 1998

Current presenter: Paddy O'Connell (@paddy_o_c)

Past presenters: Eddie Mair, Fi Glover (@fifiglover)

Listening figures: 1.9 million (weekly figures from RAJAR for the first quarter of 2014)

Description: The Sunday morning magazine programme with a fresh approach to the news, and discussion about the big stories of the week.

Website: www.bbc.co.uk/programmes/b006qnj3

Broadcasting House takes itself less seriously than other Radio 4 news programmes. Early examples of its irreverence include 'The Donald Rumsfeld Sound Bite of the Week' and 'Martin Jarvis Reads *Harry Potter and the Philosopher's Stone*', which parodied the amount of time Radio 4 was devoting to Harry Potter and to readings by Martin Jarvis.

There is a weekly quiz with a cryptic sound that is a clue to a recent news event. The prize is a honey spoon (although it was originally a jam spoon). The programme also makes frequent visits to the *Broadcasting House* beehive in south-west London.

More serious features include the headlines and the current affairs sections, which look at the background to recent news stories. There is also a review of the Sunday papers with guest reviewers.

A LITTLE 4 THOUGHT

In 2011 the BBC apologised after comedian Mike McShane used the f-word during a live newspaper review on *Broadcasting House* recorded at the Edinburgh Festival.

Portrait of the Presenter As a Listener
PADDY O'CONNELL
Presenter, *Broadcasting House*

My first memory of Radio 4 is... Brian Redhead on a bike in China ringing the bell and saying 'the sound of China'.

Radio 4 matters because... it's for people who are passionate and curious about life in this country.

FILE ON 4

PROGRAMME STATS

Running since: 1977

Presenters include: Allan Urry, Gerry Northam, Jenny Cuffe, Julian O'Halloran

Past presenters: Nick Clarke, Bridget Kendall, Robin Lustig, Winifred Robinson, Stephen Sackur, Justin Webb

Description: Award-winning current affairs documentary series investigating major issues at home and abroad.

Website: www.bbc.co.uk/programmes/b006th08

Twitter: @BBCfileon4

Is the family doctor an endangered species? How effective is the system for investigating miscarriages of justice? Modern-day slavery in the UK – how the homeless and vulnerable are used for cheap labour. These are just some of the issues tackled by the team of investigative reporters.

In 2003 the programme won a Sony Gold Award for its investigation into cot deaths, which turned up new evidence that helped to quash Sally Clark's conviction. The award judges said the programme was a 'journalistic tour de force', and 'brave, compassionate and unswerving in its sense of the injustice done'.

> 66 *Our approach is invariably sceptical,*
> *but always fair. We avoid the answers that*
> *come easily, realising that life is more*
> *complex than a sound bite.* 99
>
> **JENNY CUFFE**

ANALYSIS

PROGRAMME STATS

Running since: 1970

Presenters include: Frances Cairncross, Andrew Dilnot, Mary Goldring, Ben Hammersley, Peter Hennessy, Peter Kellner, Kenan Malik, Ian McIntyre, Robert Tyrrell

Description: Programme examining the ideas and forces which shape public policy in Britain and abroad, presented by distinguished writers, journalists and academics.

Website: www.bbc.co.uk/programmes/b006r4vz

Twitter: @BBC_Analysis

According to one of its original producers *Analysis* aimed 'to go beyond the *bien pensant* agenda'. *Analysis* presenters are journalists, academics and writers, and the current affairs issues covered by the programme are wide-ranging. The programme's website, for example, lists the following topical areas: economics, British politics, global politics, society and culture, political Islam, Europe, education, gender and identity, business and finance.

CHEERS AND TEARS

CRACKING UP

Even the most experienced Radio 4 presenters have not at all times had the gravitas you might expect of Radio 4. Here are a few of the unscripted moments that we all love so much:

In the late 1970s and early 1980s, senior newsreader Bryan Martin (1935–2009) was responsible for announcing many important events, such as the Iranian Embassy siege in 1980. But on one occasion a bulletin announcing 'Sugar shortage – Sainsbury's say there should be sufficient supplies in the shops by Saturday' sent him into fits of suppressed laughter.

Alas, the legendary giggling fit that infected the *Today* programme in 1997 pre-dates YouTube. The team that morning comprised Charlotte Green, Sue MacGregor and James Naughtie. It all started when Green had to read an item about the Papua New Guinean Chief of Staff, General Jack Tuat (pronounced 'twat'), immediately followed by a story that a 40-foot sperm whale had become stuck in the Firth of Forth. At this point she was just about managing to stifle her giggles. Next up, however, was James Naughtie, who was scheduled to do a phone interview with an angry spokesman from the Northern

Ireland Prison Officers' Association, Mr Finlay Spratt. When Naughtie inadvertently introduced him as Mr Pratt, and then let out a snort, it all fell apart, and all three presenters surrendered completely to helpless laughter. Mr Finlay Spratt's reaction is not known.

During a live news broadcast in 2008, Green suffered a highly infectious fit of the giggles while she was announcing a death. She had been set off by the previous item, which featured an 1860 recording of a woman singing 'Au Clair de la Lune', thought to be the earliest recording of a human voice. Apparently someone in the studio had remarked that it sounded like a 'bee buzzing in a bottle'.

In June 2009 weather reporter Tomasz Schafernaker was reporting on what the weather would be like for Glastonbury Festival-goers when he inadvertently predicted they would have 'quite a muddy shite'.

In 2009 Evan Davis saw the silly side of the MPs' expenses/ duck island story. Although in danger of being infected by the giggles herself, Sarah Montague gamely carried on reading the story of how 'ducks like to squeeze through a smaller opening', before admonishing Davis: 'It's serious stuff, Evan.'

For many delighted (and a few horrified) listeners, the mother of all giggling fits happened when, on a Monday morning in December 2010, James Naughtie announced that after the news they would be talking to 'Jeremy Cu... Hunt, the Culture Secretary'. There ensued a few tortuous minutes of helpless, strangulated, highly contagious laughter, while he tried to carry on doing his job.

Astonishingly, only hours later, Andrew Marr repeated the slip on *Start the Week*. *The Guardian* described it as 'like a driver slowing down to observe the wreckage of another's prang'.

An honourable mention goes here to Charlotte Green for NOT cracking up when she very well might have. In 1997, for example,

The Independent reported that when she was introducing the cast of a Radio 4 play *Heartache*, she had to announce a cast of actors playing body parts: Richard Griffiths was the Brain, Lee Montague played the Heart, Jim Broadbent was cast as the Stomach, and 'David de Keyser as the Penis'.

She also gets the prize for one of the sweetest spoonerisms, when she announced that a 'cross-flannel cherry' had been grounded on a sandbank.

CHOKING UP

From time to time even the most professional presenters become emotionally involved in the stories they are reading:

During her last transmission in 2002, Sue MacGregor was so overcome by emotion that she managed to 'crash the pips' spectacularly.

In 2013, during *Broadcasting House*, Paddy O'Connell struggled to compose himself following a reading of a love letter from Emilie Blachère to Rémi Ochlik, who died in the besieged city of Homs. O'Connell was unable to speak for a full ten seconds, and when he did his voice was choked with emotion.

In 2014 on *Woman's Hour*, Jenni Murray's guests in the studio were Doreen Lawrence and Beverley Knight. When Knight sang 'Fallen Soldier', a song she had written in memory of Stephen Lawrence (the murdered son of Doreen Lawrence), it moved both Murray and Lawrence to tears.

TALKING POLITICS – RADIO 4'S RELATIONSHIP WITH WESTMINSTER

> **❝** *It was said by Margaret Thatcher that in Downing Street a typical day began for her when Denis, having switched on* Today *in the bathroom, would wake her with cries of: 'Bastards! Bastards!'* **❞**
>
> **MICHAEL PORTILLO**

This chapter concerns 'pure' politics, if such a thing exists. Obviously there is a big overlap between this and the previous chapter, but the relationship between Radio 4 and Westminster gets its own chapter because it is a special, if sometimes dysfunctional, relationship.

BBC Radio started covering the workings of Westminster in 1945, and live broadcasting of the Lords and Commons has been permitted since 1978. The BBC's parliamentary correspondents are based at studios in Millbank in London.

Like a marriage that veers between harmony and dysfunction, it's an odd relationship that sometimes works and sometimes results in screaming rows. Politicians are both creators and consumers of news. They know that they are under a magnifying glass when they say anything on Radio 4, and they also need the oxygen of publicity for survival, particularly if they want to be perceived as serious politicians. Many report that Radio 4 is their main way of staying in touch with what's going on in their own lives.

CLASH OF THE TITANS – CHURCHILL AND REITH

Things did not get off to a good start between the BBC and politicians, and the early days of radio were coloured by the (now) well-documented antipathy between John Reith and Winston Churchill.

Churchill called Reith 'that Wuthering Height', and described the BBC as the 'enemy within the gates, doing more harm than good'. He complained bitterly about how little radio airtime he was given, but it seems his complaint was not without cause. In the decade leading up to World War Two he was heard over the airwaves just ten times – and two of them were charitable appeals.

By all accounts the real vitriol was from Reith towards Churchill. The first time the two men met, in 1926, Reith recorded in his diary that Churchill was 'really very stupid'. From there it was a slippery slope to pure hatred.

They met often, and appeared to have a working relationship. (Reith recorded: 'I was friendly and smiled and he beamed at me.') Yet Reith's dark, brooding inner world was very different, as his diaries make clear:

20 February 1940	'Churchill is a horrid fellow.'
4 December 1940	'Feeling *very* disgusted with Churchill...'
November 1941	'I absolutely hate him.'
8 October 1942	'Churchill is essentially rotten.'
1967	'That bloody shit Churchill.'

There is plenty more venom and vitriol in his diaries, although perhaps it's fair to say that Reith's antipathy towards Churchill was just one aspect of a more general hatred, as he recorded in 1941 that he was 'disgusted with politics and politicians'.

BROADCASTING PARLIAMENT

For all his antipathy towards politics and politicians, from the outset Reith wanted to broadcast Parliament. He proposed live radio coverage of the King's Speech or the Budget statement, but the idea was rejected whenever it was raised. Here is a timeline of how broadcasting Parliament was debated and eventually permitted:

1949   An inquiry advises that broadcasting proceedings would be harmful.

1950   Microphones installed in the rebuilt Commons Chamber.

1968   The Commons tries a private experiment with radio coverage, but it is deemed too expensive.

1975   MPs back a month-long public radio experiment.

1976   MPs vote for radio broadcasting on a permanent basis.

1978   The first Commons and Lords debates are broadcast live on radio.

A LITTLE **4** THOUGHT

The first broadcast from the House of Commons was of the Secretary of State for Wales answering questions on the Welsh language.

When he got to his feet in 1968 amid enthusiastic applause to address a large Labour Party Conference audience in Blackpool, Harold Wilson opened with the wry observation: 'Thank you for what the BBC, if they're true to their usual form, will tonight describe as a hostile reception.'

TODAY IN PARLIAMENT

PROGRAMME STATS

Running since: 1945

Current presenters: Sean Curran (@cripeswatson), Mark D'Arcy (@DArcyTiP), Susan Hulme (@Susanh12) and others

Description: A daily round-up of the most significant stories in Parliament.

Related programme: *Yesterday in Parliament* (LW only)

Website: www.bbc.co.uk/programmes/b006qtqd

WEEK IN WESTMINSTER

PROGRAMME STATS

Running since: 2007

Current presenters: Fronted by a journalist, often from the world of print journalism.

Description: Radio 4's weekly assessment of developments at Westminster.

Website: www.bbc.co.uk/programmes/b006qjfq

The *Week in Westminster* counts among its alumni Guy Burgess, later revealed as a Soviet double agent. Burgess worked for the BBC between 1936 and 1944 – getting to know many members of the British establishment along the way.

A BBC internal memo dated 20 April 1943 and signed by G. J. B. Allport expresses concern about Burgess's 'activities in general' while he was producer of the *Week in Westminster*. But rather than espionage, the concern turns out to be connected with the amount he was spending on entertaining MPs in the BBC bar in order to persuade them to appear on the programme, and his habit of loaning the services of BBC secretaries out to MPs.

ANY QUESTIONS?

PROGRAMME STATS

Running since: 1948

Current presenter: Jonathan Dimbleby (since 1987)

Past presenters: Freddie Grisewood (1948–1967), David Jacobs (1967–1984), John Timpson (1984–1987)

Description: Topical discussion in which a panel of personalities from the worlds of politics, media and elsewhere are posed questions by the audience. From a different location each week.

Related programme: *Any Answers?*

Website: www.bbc.co.uk/programmes/b006qgvj

Frank Gillard originally created the *Any Questions?* format for the BBC West region. It was first broadcast from the Guildhall in Winchester, when one of the questions was whether Britain should reintroduce rations.

In the autumn of 1956, *Any Questions?* was at the cutting edge of the row between broadcasters and the government during the Suez Crisis. On 2 November Freddie Grisewood opened the programme by announcing that the question that had been overwhelmingly asked by the audience '… cannot be dealt with in this programme because of the fourteen-day rule'. The rule in question prohibited broadcasters from discussing any matter until two weeks after Parliament had discussed it. There was instant uproar, and the ensuing programme revolved around the non-discussion.

When Enoch Powell was on the panel in 1976, protesters threw bricks at the church in Basingstoke where it was being recorded. Presenter David Jacobs led the panel off the platform – and back 10 minutes later when the police had re-established order.

A LITTLE 4 THOUGHT

Tony Benn first appeared as a panel member in 1951 and contributed to over eighty programmes – a record he holds posthumously.

WESTMINSTER HOUR

PROGRAMME STATS

Running since: 1998

Current presenter: Carolyn Quinn (since 2006)

Past presenter: Andrew Rawnsley (1998–2006)

Description: Radio 4's Sunday night political discussion programme.

Website: www.bbc.co.uk/programmes/b006s624

Twitter: @BBCWestminHour

BBC NEWS POLITICAL EDITORS

1981–1992	John Cole
1992–2000	Robin Oakley
2000–2005	Andrew Marr
2005–present	Nick Robinson (@bbcnickrobinson)

THINGS YOU (PROBABLY) NEVER KNEW ABOUT BBC NEWS POLITICAL EDITORS

Nick Robinson's interest in politics and journalism was inspired by author, journalist and broadcaster Brian Redhead, the father of his best friend Will Redhead.

In 2014, while he was in the middle of a heated live debate on BBC Two about bankers' bonuses, Nick Robinson's iPad suddenly interrupted with Queen's hit 'Fat-bottomed Girls'.

At Oxford, Nick Robinson was president of the University Conservative Association.

At Cambridge, Andrew Marr was a self-confessed 'raving leftie'. Known as 'Red Andy', he was a Maoist and used to give out copies of the *Little Red Book*.

Robin Oakley relates that Jeffrey Archer once said to him that the world is divided into those who know how to make money and those who don't: 'You, Robin, are in the second category.'

John Cole's *Spitting Image* puppet wore a tin hat, was incomprehensible and often talked for so long that the other puppets were seen falling asleep.

When an IRA bomb exploded at the Grand Hotel in Brighton during the Conservative Party Conference in 1984, John Cole was still recovering from major heart surgery. The next time he was in touch with the hospital shortly afterwards, staff censured him for working too hard, having seen him interview Margaret Thatcher at night-time.

ELECTION CALL

Since 1979 the phone-in programme *Election Call* has been broadcast on Radio 4 each day in the run-up to a General Election. Callers are able to put questions to senior politicians live on air.

It was presented by Robin Day, then Jonathan Dimbleby, and has developed a reputation for being 'the programme most likely to trip up politicians'.

In 1979 Margaret Thatcher was challenged by a caller to defend her use of the term 'swamped' in connection with immigration. The lady was, as the expression goes, not for turning, and swept to power shortly after.

For a while attempts were made to up the ante in terms of interactivity. From 1983 *Election Call* started to be simulcasted on BBC One, and web broadcasting and email were also introduced. By the General Election of 2010, however, the programme had returned to a straightforward phone-in show.

Portrait of the Politician As a Listener
MICHAEL PORTILLO
Former Conservative MP and Cabinet Minister

My first memory of the Home Service is... Jack de Manio on the *Today* programme frequently getting the time wrong.

When I'm not working I listen to... I listen to R4 almost exclusively in the morning: *Tweet of the Day*, *Farming Today*, *From Our Own Correspondent*, *Start the Week*, *In Our Time* (the best programme on Radio 4), but above all else, *Today*. I listen to *Today* wherever I am in the world on my iPhone. Most of my news comes from *Today*, ahead of newspapers and online sources. That has always been the case for me, so it must have hugely influenced my political career.

Portrait of the Politician As a Listener
HILARY BENN
Labour MP For Leeds Central

When I'm not working I listen to... *Today, Just a Minute* and *The News Quiz.*

Portrait of the Politician As a Listener
CAROLINE LUCAS
Green Party MP For Brighton Pavilion

My first memory of Radio 4 is... the theme tune to *The Archers* signalling the time I had to go to bed – it was when it was on at 6.45, and I would have been about eight or nine years old. Radio 4 has been a constant presence all of my life – always on in the early evening when I was growing up (listening to programmes like *Just a Minute* over supper, before *The Archers*), and always on at home now. I use it to tell the time by – be up by 7.30 a.m. news, in bed before the end of the *Shipping Forecast.*

Radio 4 programmes I listen to include... *Poetry Please*, *Woman's Hour*, *Start the Week* and the *Shipping Forecast*, as well as the more obvious *Today* programme and *Today in Parliament* (and I still catch *The Archers* on Sundays sometimes).

Radio 4 matters because... of its authority, and its extraordinary breadth and scope. I particularly appreciate the way it takes the arts seriously but not pompously. I love the late-night comedy shows too.

WEEK ENDING

Week Ending merits inclusion in the chapter on politics because, despite the variety of its content, it developed a reputation as a thorn in the side of the politicians. So much so that, until 1983, the show was taken off air during election campaigns for fear of damaging parties' reputations. Eventually it was allowed to remain during the 1987, 1992 and 1997 elections, although still closely monitored.

Despite all that, it ran for twenty-eight years, from 1970 to 1998, and 1,132 editions were broadcast.

Devised by writer–producers Simon Brett and David Hatch, it was originally presented by *Nationwide* presenter Michael Barratt. It is generally agreed (including by Barratt himself) that it was an uneasy fit for a news presenter to be presenting a satirical current affairs show.

It wasn't quite the case, as has been claimed, that anyone could walk into a *Week Ending* script meeting in the 1980s, although there was a big push to recruit new talent, and non-commissioned writers' meetings were held regularly. Consequently, *Week Ending* was a hothouse of comedy talent.

Among those who cut their teeth on comedy as writers, performers or producers on the programme were: Douglas Adams, Colin Bostock-Smith, Steve Coogan, Andy Hamilton, Jeremy Hardy, Harry Hill, Armando Iannucci, David Jason, John Lloyd, Alistair McGowan, Andy Parsons, Ged Parsons, Iain Pattinson, Richard Herring, Stewart Lee, Jimmy Mulville, Al Murray, Griff Rhys Jones, Alison Steadman and Tracey Ullman.

A LITTLE 4 THOUGHT

Harry Hill was running a cardiology and diabetes clinic at a London hospital when he began faxing jokes to *Week Ending* from a machine that was supposed to be kept clear for alerts of donor-matching organs.

TODAY

PROGRAMME STATS

Running since: 1957

Current presenters: Evan Davis (@EvanHD), John Humphrys (since 1987), Mishal Husain (@MishalHusainBBC), Sarah Montague (@Sarah_Montague), James Naughtie (@naughtiej), Justin Webb (@JustinOnWeb)

Some past presenters: Jack de Manio (1958–1971), John Timpson (1970–1976, 1978–1986), Robert Robinson (1971–1974), Barry Norman (1974–1976), Desmond Lynam (1974–1976), Brian Redhead (1975–1993), Gillian Reynolds (1976), Nigel Rees (1976–1978), Libby Purves (1978–1981), Jenni Murray (1985–1987), Sue MacGregor (1984–2002), Anna Ford (1989–1997), Edward Stourton (1999–2009), Carolyn Quinn (2004–2008)

Listening figures: 7.06 million (weekly figures from RAJAR for the first quarter of 2014)

Description: Radio 4's flagship news and current affairs programme; including religious reflections from *Thought for the Day* at 7.48 a.m.

Website: www.bbc.co.uk/programmes/b006qj9z

For most of us who aren't farmers, our first daily contact with Radio 4 – or indeed with any other human voice – is the *Today* programme. For seven million people it's as much a part of the early morning ritual as a mug of tea.

Over the years *Today* has become an institution, but it has evolved almost beyond recognition from the programme it was when it was introduced in 1957, billed as a light-hearted look at the news. The 'erratic' Jack de Manio was a colourful presenter in those early days – famously incompetent at telling the time – but he did little to move the programme towards being the serious news and current affairs programme it is today.

As late as the early 1970s, BBC World Affairs Editor John Simpson remarked that no one accused *Today* of dumbing down, 'because it was pretty dumbed-down already'.

Things didn't improve much when, in 1977 and 1978, Radio 4 controller Ian McIntyre controversially cut the programme in two, and placed a light magazine show called *Up to the Hour* in the middle of its time slot. Presenters and listeners alike were scathing about the innovation, with programme editor Mike Chaney describing it as 'absolute crap, the floor-sweepings', and Libby Purves remembering that it was 'desperately demoralising... a kind of physical pain to have to stop for *Up to the Hour* each day'.

A LITTLE 4 THOUGHT

The story goes that on one occasion, just as *Today* was beginning, Jack de Manio shoved his notes over to colleague Tim Matthews and hurried from the studio. Gamely, Matthews picked up the notes and embarked upon a rather serious story about a plane hijack, only to be interrupted by de Manio returning to the studio and apologetically announcing live on air that he'd been 'stuck in the loo'.

It was once announced that the following day's *Today* would be an outside broadcast from an undisclosed location. Listeners tuning in the following morning may have been disappointed to discover that the location in question was a hole in the road outside Broadcasting House.

John Timpson became famous for slipping humour and puns into his reports, with announcements such as 'Insulation – Britain lags behind', or 'Crash course for learner drivers'.

DOWN THE LINE

In 1988 an earthquake in Armenia caused President Gorbachev to cancel his visit to Britain. Shortly after it had been reported on *Today*, Margaret Thatcher called the programme live from 10 Downing Street, to the obvious surprise of John Humphrys.

She started 'Hello, good morning', before going on to explain that she had first heard the news on *Today* herself: '... I heard later that you didn't know whether I'd heard, so I thought I'd better let you know I had.'

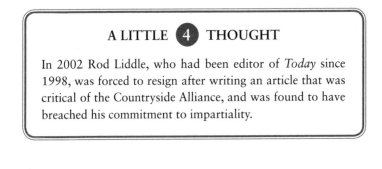

A LITTLE 4 THOUGHT

In 2002 Rod Liddle, who had been editor of *Today* since 1998, was forced to resign after writing an article that was critical of the Countryside Alliance, and was found to have breached his commitment to impartiality.

TODAY AND HUTTON

If *Today* had lacked gravitas in the early days, things became really serious in May 2003, when a report by Defence Correspondent Andrew Gilligan quoted a government official as having said that a dossier concerning weapons of mass destruction in Iraq had been 'sexed up'. Alastair Campbell was implicated in a newspaper report, and Ministry of Defence scientist Dr David Kelly was named as the alleged source of the story.

In the furore following Dr Kelly's suicide in July 2003, and following the publication of the Hutton Report in January 2004, the BBC was severely censured, prompting the resignation of both BBC Chairman Gavyn Davies and Director General Greg Dyke, followed by Gilligan himself.

A LITTLE 4 THOUGHT

In 2006 a copy of the Hutton Report, signed by Cherie Blair, was auctioned for £400 in aid of the Labour Party – a move which was condemned in a House of Commons motion as 'appalling bad taste'.

MAKING THE NEWS

John Humphrys' interview with BBC Director General George Entwistle on 11 November 2012 is widely credited with having been a major factor in Entwistle's resignation later the same day.

It followed the scandal in which an edition of *Newsnight* claimed that a 'senior Conservative' was guilty of child abuse. Although Lord McAlpine was not named, the ensuing frenzy of speculation and accusation on Twitter and other social media led to the BBC being criticised, and ultimately to Entwistle's on-air drubbing by Humphrys. Although Entwistle claimed he was not aware of the story, making a statement that 'not every piece of journalism made inside the BBC is referred to the editor-in-chief', he later stepped down with the acknowledgement that, as Director General and editor-in-chief, he was ultimately responsible for all content. McAlpine's accuser retracted all his allegations against him.

A LITTLE 4 THOUGHT

In 2011 it was reported that only 16.6 per cent of reporters and guests on the show were female. A year later this proportion had risen to 18.5 per cent.

GUEST EDITORS

It seems that today's *Today* listeners are very sensitive to any hint of dumbing down or straying from the format. When in January 2014 musician PJ Harvey was invited to guest-edit an edition, her intention was to shake up the format and give airtime to people whose voices are not often heard.

Accordingly, she invited radical journalist John Pilger and WikiLeaks founder Julian Assange, among others, to contribute. Critics on all sides were scathing about what they regarded as 'tosh', 'drivel' and 'claptrap'. One notable exception was Labour MP Diane Abbott, who said Harvey should 'do it every day'.

A LITTLE **4** THOUGHT

Aside from PJ Harvey, guest editors of the *Today* programme have included Barclays Bank chief Antony Jenkins, former MI5 Director Eliza Manningham-Buller, explorer and Python Michael Palin, and inventor of the World Wide Web Sir Tim Berners-Lee.

BONO! YOU'RE LIVE ON THE *TODAY* PROGRAMME!

Just a couple of months after PJ Harvey's edition of *Today*, the presenting style of Colin Paterson, whose regular stamping-ground is Radio 5 Live, was likened to that of Alan Partridge when he appeared on the programme. As he pointed out later, he had been seconded to the *Today* programme without prior warning to cover *Vanity Fair*'s Oscars party. On seeing Bono walk by, he 'went back into a Radio 5 moment', yelling 'Bono!

Bono! Bono – you're live on the *Today* programme!' before forgetting whether it was John Humphrys or James Naughtie he was speaking to back in the studio. Paterson later admitted it was 'not the finest moment of my career'.

TURNING THE AIRWAVES BLUE

On a Friday morning in July 2011 listeners tuning into *Today* shortly after 8 a.m. were treated to a catalogue of expletives, when the words 'bullshit' and 'bastards' were repeatedly used during a recorded item.

The item in question was about a report that academics researching chronic fatigue syndrome, or ME, had been sent emails claiming their research was 'bullshit' and calling them 'evil bastards'.

This led to calls by Mediawatch-UK for á radio 'watershed' to be introduced, which a spokesperson for the *Today* programme responded to by saying, 'Emails including abusive language were included in the report to demonstrate the level of intimidation involved in the campaign. We felt this was editorially justified.'

A LITTLE 4 THOUGHT

When it comes to matters of 'decency', there is no 'watershed' policy for radio as for television. The BBC guidelines state: 'Radio is a different medium with different audiences, so we cannot operate a similar watershed policy.'

REDHEAD SEES RED

In 1987, Brian Redhead interviewed the Chancellor Nigel Lawson and challenged him over unemployment. When Lawson dismissed his comments as those of 'a lifelong Labour supporter', Redhead asked for a minute's silence 'while you compose an apology for daring to suggest you know how I exercise my vote'.

THINGS YOU (PROBABLY) NEVER KNEW ABOUT *TODAY* PRESENTERS PAST AND PRESENT

John Humphrys has played himself twice in film and television: in a 2013 crime thriller entitled *Closed Circuit*, and in a 2014 television comedy, *The Life of Rock with Brian Pern*.

On Red Nose Day 2009 Jo Brand told Sarah Montague that she didn't need to wear a red nose because she had a drink problem. Montague took it in good humour.

Evan Davis is rumoured to have some interesting piercings.

In 2011 Justin Webb revealed that his biological father was newsreader Peter Woods, who had had an affair with his mother. Woods presented the first colour news programme on British television in 1967.

You can buy Barry Norman's Premium Pickled Onions – made from a recipe that has been passed down for generations in his family.

66 Today *isn't today without* Today! **99**
JAMES HARRISON, CAMPSITE MANAGER

DRAMA AND READINGS

THE EARLY DAYS – DRAMA IN THE DARK

In the first year of BBC Radio's existence, drama was confined to reading extracts from Shakespeare and a bit of entertainment for children. Then, in January 1924, the first full play ever to be commissioned and written specifically for radio was broadcast on the BBC. It was seen as a radical experiment and nobody really knew whether it would work.

This, it has to be remembered, was a full three years before the release of the first feature-length talkie film. In those days radio drama – sound without pictures – was thought of as the 'missing half' of the silent film – pictures without sound.

The 'listening play' in question was *A Comedy of Danger* by Richard Hughes, who apparently wrote it overnight. Because it was thought to be a significant problem that there was nothing to see, Hughes came up with the brilliant idea of setting his drama in a coal mine after a collapse.

As producer Nigel Playfair pointed out, had it been a stage play: 'the stage would have been in total darkness; the players and the action would remain unseen.' He concluded that *A Comedy of Danger* 'was, therefore, ideal for broadcasting'.

This was the era of coconut shells for horses' hooves, and Playfair was having to make it up as he went along. In order to approximate the sound of being below ground, it's said that he made the actors speak their lines with their heads in buckets. Meanwhile the Welsh choir performed out in the corridor in order to create a sense of distance.

On the night itself, the audience was advised to listen in darkness – and in homes all around the country, people turned the lights off before settling down around the wireless.

Happily, the experiment worked, and the following day's *Daily Mail* gave the play a thumbs up with the headline 'Drama Thrills by Wireless'.

A LITTLE **4** THOUGHT

Another first for *A Comedy of Danger* was the broadcasting of the first Welsh-language words on radio, when some trapped miners were heard singing 'Ar Hyd y Nos' ('All Through the Night').

In the early days all radio drama was live. Famously, a live production of *Hamlet* was overrunning: as Hamlet's fatal duel moved towards the pips, the action faded and a voice announced in a cut-glass BBC accent '… and there we must leave Elsinore.'

VAL GIELGUD (1900–1981)

Val Gielgud was a pioneer of radio drama during its formative period. As well as a broadcaster, he was a prolific author and, like his more famous brother John, an actor.

Gielgud came to BBC drama through working at the *Radio Times*, although it would appear that he had always craved more direct involvement in drama. Years later, he would confess that during his time at the *Radio Times* he had made up a number of the listeners' letters which were critical of the way BBC drama was managed.

In 1929, despite never having directed a radio play, he was appointed Head of Variety with responsibility for all BBC radio drama. At last, it seems, he had his chance to roll up his sleeves and get really involved in drama. By all accounts he grasped the opportunity, and went on to work in television drama also during its formative years, directing the first drama ever aired on the BBC. Most critics, however, would agree that his main contribution was to radio drama.

DEATH AT BROADCASTING HOUSE

The 1934 film *Death at Broadcasting House* was a murder mystery based on a novel written by Val Gielgud. In the 'drama within a drama' an actor is strangled while delivering his lines for a live radio drama. The film is said to replicate the exact layout of Broadcasting House, and to be a very accurate representation of radio production techniques at the time. For example, it was common for actors to say their lines in individual studios, so the actor's isolation enabled the murderer to strike while he was on air portraying a man being strangled. The film also shows a five-piece music ensemble providing the live music between scenes.

THE FEATURES DEPARTMENT

Although it was an age of technological experimentation, Gielgud's department was essentially producing theatre in the fairly traditional sense. Meanwhile, another department at BBC Radio, the Features Department, was pushing the boundaries in terms of form and content.

Why the Features Department was so called is not clear, but its vague remit gave the writers and producers who worked there space to chuck everything into the mix and see what came out. The result was an eclectic fusion of drama, history, poetry and documentary.

As might be expected, the department attracted innovators and radicals. Producer R. D. 'Reggie' Smith, for example, was a paid-up member of the Communist Party who was being watched by MI5 as a possible spy.

Among the writer–producers in the department were a number of poets, most notably the Irish poet and playwright Louis MacNeice, who was employed at the BBC in 1941 when his poor eyesight prevented him from joining the war effort. During his time at the Features Department he wrote and/or produced over seventy dramas, including *Christopher Columbus* (1942) and *The Dark Tower* (1946).

THE POST-WAR YEARS

Notwithstanding their different approaches, innovators such as Playfair, Gielgud, Smith and MacNeice developed and nurtured drama in the early days of BBC Radio. In the post-war period the genre grew in stature (with highbrow drama generally broadcast on the Third Programme, forerunner to Radio 3), and gave airtime to some really innovative writers.

Among those who contributed to the genre were Dorothy L. Sayers (*The Man Born to Be King*, 1941), Dylan Thomas (*Under*

Milk Wood, 1954) and Samuel Beckett (*All that Fall*, 1957). It was on BBC Radio that Joe Orton got his big break with *The Ruffian on the Stair* (1964).

Other writers who have come to attention writing for BBC Radio drama include Caryl Churchill, Lee Hall, Christopher Hampton, Harold Pinter, Tom Stoppard and Rose Tremain, while actors whose voices have graced the airwaves include Peggy Ashcroft, Richard Burton, Judi Dench, John Gielgud, Paul Scofield – and, of course, many, many more.

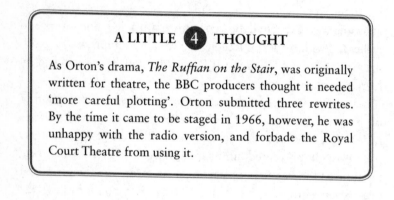

A LITTLE 4 THOUGHT

As Orton's drama, *The Ruffian on the Stair*, was originally written for theatre, the BBC producers thought it needed 'more careful plotting'. Orton submitted three rewrites. By the time it came to be staged in 1966, however, he was unhappy with the radio version, and forbade the Royal Court Theatre from using it.

THE REP

The BBC's Radio Drama Company, known as the Rep, was founded in 1940 and still continues to offer upwards of thirty young actors the opportunity to hone their skills in radio drama, while at the same time providing BBC producers with a 'pool' of talent they can tap into. Among its alumni are Emma Fielding, Richard Griffiths, Edward Kelsey (*The Archers*' Joe Grundy), Julian Rhind-Tutt and Stephen Tompkinson.

THE CURRENT STATE OF PLAY

Drama is of course a well-established part of the Radio 4 schedule now, with listeners devoted to particular strands. With drama, as with everything Radio 4, all life is here. Tune in on any weekday when a drama or reading is airing, and you might hear biography, classics, period drama, crime, history, horror, legal drama, music, politics, psychology, romance, sci-fi and fantasy, soaps, thrillers, the drama of war – or a combination of any or all of the above.

Of course, as with everything on Radio 4, the listener has a sense of ownership over it and never holds back from speaking out. When in 2010 it was announced that the *Friday Play* was to be cut, it provoked uproar – not just from listeners, but from actors, agents, writers and producers. They argued that the hour-long 9–10 p.m. weekly slot was one of the last bastions of really cutting-edge drama which gave airtime to controversial or difficult subjects.

Among the dramas that had been aired was Philip Ralph's *Deep Cut*, which had dealt with the death of eighteen-year-old Private Cheryl James at the Deepcut army barracks in 1995.

These days Radio 4's Drama Department is responsible for commissioning over three hundred drama and readings titles a year. Not all the department's output is drama, strictly speaking, and the *Book of the Week* readings are always works of non-fiction.

Radio 4's main drama strands are:

Afternoon Drama
15-minute Drama (previously the *Woman's Hour Drama*)
Classic Serial
Saturday Drama

Readings include:

Book of the Week (non-fiction)
Afternoon Reading
Book at Bedtime

A LITTLE **4** THOUGHT

Under Milk Wood was originally broadcast on BBC Radio in 1954, and then again in a new recording in 1963. Both productions starred Richard Burton as 'First Voice'. In November 2003, to mark the fiftieth anniversary of Dylan Thomas's death, Radio 4 broadcast a new production. The use of digital noise-reduction technology meant that contemporary actors could be heard alongside the 1963 cast.

AFTERNOON DRAMA

PROGRAMME STATS

Running since: 1967

Description: Radio dramas which delight and surprise.

Website: www.bbc.co.uk/programmes/b006qrzz

Radio 4's flagship drama strand was titled *Afternoon Play* until 2012. In one form or another it has been a feature of Radio 4 since its launch, although the standard forty-five-minute format was not introduced until 1998, when the play was moved to its current time slot after *The Archers*.

Most of the dramas are self-contained plays, although there are also short series (of generally two to six episodes). From time to time the *Afternoon Drama* will include an adaptation of a popular work such as Alexander McCall Smith's *The No. 1 Ladies' Detective Agency*.

Listening figures for the *Afternoon Drama* are around the one million mark, making it one of the most popular outlets for new dramatic writing in the world.

A LITTLE **4** THOUGHT

Several *Afternoon Plays* were among the programmes produced in underground radio stations by the BBC's Wartime Broadcasting Service, which was established during World War Two, the idea being that it would provide public information and morale-boosting broadcasts for 100 days after a nuclear attack. The studios and transmitter were deactivated in 1993, but the government still has the legal right to take over the airways in the event of a national emergency.

BOOK AT BEDTIME

PROGRAMME STATS

Running since: 1949

Description: Readings from modern classics, new works by leading writers and literature from around the world.

Website: www.bbc.co.uk/programmes/b006qtlx

Ever since *The Three Hostages* by John Buchan was broadcast on 21 January 1949, *Book at Bedtime* has been a feature of the BBC Radio airwaves. Typically, a *Book at Bedtime* is an abridged novel that takes between one and three weeks to read in fourteen-minute instalments.

It might be a modern classic, a new work by a leading novelist, a novel by an up-and-coming writer, or a little-known work by a classic author, for example Jane Austen's *Lady Susan*. From time to time some short stories from a collection will be read consecutively.

The works of world-renowned writers, such as Daphne du Maurier, F. Scott Fitzgerald, Ian Fleming, Georgette Heyer, John le Carré, Ian McEwan, Michael Palin and Muriel Spark have been read for *Book at Bedtime*, while their words have been read by a glittering cast of actors – among them Niamh Cusack, Dawn French, David Jason, Bill Nighy and Stephen Rea.

In spite of its cosy, mumsy title, *Book at Bedtime* is capable of controversy, and it doesn't always tuck us up with a soothing story to send us peacefully on our way into the land of nod. In 2008, commissioning editor Caroline Raphael came under fire for including Canadian writer Barbara Gowdy's *Helpless*, which tells how a repairman stalks and abducts a nine-year-old girl. Listeners contacted *Feedback* to say it was 'inappropriate', 'disturbing' and 'tasteless'. Raphael responded that the book was 'extremely well written' and also suggested that 'people had a choice for 14 minutes to turn off the radio if they didn't want to listen to it.'

A LITTLE 4 THOUGHT

In 1990, thirty years after the 1960 trial in which Penguin Books was tried under the Obscene Publications Act and found not guilty, the unexpurgated (though abridged) *Lady Chatterley's Lover* featured on *Book at Bedtime*.

BOOK OF THE WEEK
PROGRAMME STATS

Description: Serialised book readings, featuring works of non-fiction, biography, autobiography, travel, diaries, essays, humour and history.

Website: www.bbc.co.uk/programmes/b006qftk

What do Harry Nilsson, lemons, Charles Dickens, hot air balloons, John F. Kennedy, Sweden, Cleopatra, Dizzee Rascal and pink saris have in common? Answer: they have all been the topics of *Book of the Week*.

Featured works have included Jung Chang's *Empress Dowager Cixi*, Richard Holmes's quirky account of two balloonists two hundred years apart, *Falling Upwards*, and Solomon Northup's autobiographical masterpiece *Twelve Years a Slave*.

   66 *Listening to #bookoftheweek archives –
everything you've never heard of suddenly
becomes a listening imperative.* **99**

TWITTER

DRAMA LANDMARKS

There follows a brief rundown of some landmark dramas to have graced the airwaves since Radio 4 came into existence.

THE HITCHHIKER'S GUIDE TO THE GALAXY

If you're in the know – or want to appear that you are – you might call it 'HG2G'. Douglas Adams' cult science-fiction radio series was originally broadcast from 1978 to 1980 and then, well, let's just say it went viral before the term had been coined.

To date it has been translated into over thirty languages, and spin-offs include a stage show, a five-book 'trilogy', a sixth novel (2009) by Eoin Colfer, a television series (1981), a computer game (1984), comic-book adaptations and a series of towels that are particularly prized.

A Hollywood film was released in 2005, while radio adaptations of the third, fourth and fifth novels were broadcast between 2004 and 2005. All from a humble radio show.

The series follows the adventures of the hapless Arthur Dent, who is one of the only two survivors of the demolition of planet Earth (to make way for a hyperspace bypass). He spends the next few years being buffeted around the galaxy in a state of bewilderment, still wearing his dressing gown and looking for a decent cup of tea.

A LITTLE 4 THOUGHT

Most of the sound effects for HG2G were provided by Paddy Kingsland of the legendary BBC Radiophonic Workshop, the BBC's sound effects unit which existed between 1958 and 1998.

THE LORD OF THE RINGS

Originally adapted for BBC Radio as a twelve-part drama in 1955 and 1956, in 1981 Radio 4 serialised J. R. R. Tolkein's epic masterpiece into twenty-six half-hour instalments. The glittering cast included:

Simon Cadell Celeborn
Ian Holm Frodo
Michael Hordern Gandalf
Bill Nighy Sam Gamgee
Robert Stephens Aragorn
John Le Mesurier Bilbo Baggins

Each episode was recorded in a day and a half. It was one of the first Radio 4 programmes to be transmitted in stereo and went out twice a week, with one instalment airing at Sunday lunchtime.

Although at first it received mixed reviews in the press, fans of the trilogy were convinced, and before long cassette tapes of episodes were being traded through fanzines. Stephen Oliver's theme music also proved popular, and was later released in its own right.

> 66 *Radio is Hobbit 4 ming.*
> *Get into good Radio 4 hobbits.* 99
> **BADGES SOLD WITH THE *RADIO TIMES* IN 1981**

A LITTLE 4 THOUGHT

In 1981 actress Kathryn Hurlbutt was dividing her time between Middle-earth and Ambridge, as she was playing both Rosie (Sam's wife) in *The Lord of the Rings*, and Julie the barmaid from The Bull.

In 1980, the year before his role in *The Lord of the Rings*, John Le Mesurier played the Wise Old Bird in *The Hitchhiker's Guide to the Galaxy*.

ADRIAN MOLE

A surprise hit, Adrian Mole first hit the airwaves in 1982 when he was played by the young actor Nicholas Barnes.

Nigel (later Adrian) Mole is growing up in Leicester in the early 1980s, against the backdrop of the Falklands War and the wedding of Charles and Diana – slap bang in the middle of the Thatcher years, in other words. The young self-styled intellectual is one of Thatcher's fiercest, if most impotent, critics.

For many listeners, the 1982 radio play was the beginning of a long friendship with Adrian Mole, accompanying him (in print) through his rites of passage – *The Secret Diary of Adrian Mole, Aged 13¾*, *The Growing Pains of Adrian Mole*, *True Confessions of Adrian Albert Mole*, *Adrian Mole: The Wilderness Years*, *Adrian Mole: The Cappuccino Years*, *Adrian Mole and the Weapons of Mass Destruction*, *The Lost Diaries of Adrian Mole, 1999–2001* and *Adrian Mole: The Prostrate Years*.

> 66 *Really sad to hear of the passing of Sue Townsend. The Secret Diary of Adrian Mole blew my mind when I was a teenager. I still read it. Genius.* 99
>
> **SUSAN CALMAN, TWITTER, APRIL 2014**

A LITTLE 4 THOUGHT

Adrian Albert Mole was called Nigel Mole in the 1982 Radio 4 drama, and was 13¼.

BOMBER

In 1995 Radio 4 broadcast an innovative 'real-time' dramatisation of Len Deighton's 'documentary' novel *Bomber*, starring Tom Baker (as the narrator), Frank Windsor and Sam West.

Covering 24 hours, Deighton's novel tells the story of an RAF bombing raid on Germany in 1943, focusing on the experiences of the bomber crew, the civilians in the town they bomb, and the crew sent out against them.

Echoing the novel's structure, the Radio 4 broadcast took place over a twenty-four-hour period, and was woven in among the daily schedule between early morning and midnight. It was repeated on Radio 4 Extra on Armistice Day 2011.

SPOONFACE STEINBERG

Actress Becky Simpson was only eleven when she played a seven-year-old autistic girl dying of cancer. Related as a dramatic monologue, it would have been a stretch for any actor, let alone one so young. Yet Becky pulled it off, and Lee Hall's play changed the face of radio drama.

First broadcast on Monday, 27 January 1997 it was not, in fact, originally intended to be a standalone drama, but was the fourth and final instalment of the *God's Country* series. Such was the popular acclaim that Radio 4 responded to public pressure and repeated it the following Saturday afternoon.

A LITTLE 4 THOUGHT

On Boxing Day 2000 Radio 4 cleared the schedule for a marathon eight-hour reading of *Harry Potter and the Philosopher's Stone*, read by Stephen Fry.

THE LAST ADVENTURE

One of John Mortimer's last original works before he died was written for and broadcast on Radio 4 in October 2005. Produced by his son Jeremy, *The Last Adventure* starred Michael Sheen as Lord Byron, and was set in 1824 during the last months of Byron's life.

It portrayed Byron fighting for Greek independence from Ottoman rule. Having set out to fight for freedom in the face of fascism and tyranny, Byron encountered a distinct lack of heroism among the unruly Greeks he was commanding, yet kept pouring his resources into the mission. In the end he caught the fever which would kill him in the swamps of Missolonghi.

LIFE AND FATE

In September 2011 Radio 4 broadcast an eight-hour, thirteen-part dramatisation of *Life and Fate*, a book by Vasily Grossman.

Described as an 'epic masterpiece', *Life and Fate* centres around the Battle of Stalingrad, charting the fate of both a nation and a family in the turmoil of war.

The Radio 4 adaptation starred Kenneth Branagh as the nuclear physicist Viktor Shtrum, alongside performances from Greta Scacchi, Janet Suzman and Harriet Walter.

A LITTLE 4 THOUGHT

When it was originally published in 1960, the KGB felt so threatened by *Life and Fate* that the book itself was arrested. It wasn't published in the West until 1980, and had to wait until 1988 for publication in the Soviet Union.

ULYSSES

In 2012 *The Guardian* described Radio 4's dramatisation of James Joyce's epic stream-of-consciousness novel *Ulysses* as 'the very epitome of Radio 4 flamboyance'.

Eschewing the 'dirty' bits, Radio 4's heavily abridged version was under 8 hours long. Henry Goodman played Leopold Bloom, with Niamh Cusack as his unfaithful wife Molly and Andrew Scott as Stephen Dedalus.

THE EXORCIST

In 2014 eyebrows were raised at the decision to broadcast a two-part dramatisation of *The Exorcist*. Like the film, the radio adaptation was based on the book by William Peter Blatty and dealt with the demonic possession of a young girl named Regan.

When producer and director Gaynor Macfarlane was asked how she would deal with the 'head-swivelling' scene on radio, she said: 'Our version may not have these filmic tricks, but it has a gradual, creeping, perhaps more toxic horror.'

THE ARCHERS

PROGRAMME STATS

Running since: 1950

Listening figures: 4.92 million (weekly figures from RAJAR for the first quarter of 2014)

Description: An everyday story of country folk.

Website: www.bbc.co.uk/programmes/b006qpgr

Twitter: @BBCTheArchers

What is it about *The Archers* that gets people all over the country rushing to their radios and remote controls at just after 7 p.m. each weekday evening? Admittedly a small proportion are hurrying to turn *off* the theme tune they find so irritating – but the vast majority are eager to get their daily fix of 'an everyday story of country folk'.

WHAT, NO SOAP?

Until 1950 there was one notable absence on the Home Service airwaves – the soap opera. BBC Head of Drama Val Gielgud considered soaps to be antithetical to the corporation's commitment to quality. During the war, however, they were found to be useful ways to disseminate information to the public. So reluctantly Gielgud was compelled to include soaps such as *Front Line Family* and *Dick Barton: Special Agent* in the schedule, but he confined them to the Light Programme.

Until, that is, *The Archers* burst onto the scene and changed the face of radio drama forever...

Appropriately enough, given its agricultural theme, credit for the original idea of *The Archers* goes to a Lincolnshire farmer named Henry Burtt. An expert on seed crops, leading NFU member and government adviser, in 1948 Burtt attended a Birmingham conference held by the BBC, to brainstorm ways in which they could engage farmers' attention while promoting good agricultural practice. This was in the interest of keeping the nation fed at a time when it was still in the grips of post-war food rationing.

Towards the end of the day, Burtt announced: 'What we farmers want is a farming Dick Barton.' *Dick Barton: Special Agent* was a hugely popular detective radio drama which aired on the BBC Light Programme, its cliffhanger endings keeping millions of listeners in suspense, eagerly tuning in again for the next day's instalment. His idea was taken on, as were the *Dick Barton* writers.

The Archers pilot was aired on the BBC Midlands Service on 29 May 1950, and went national on 1 January 1951. Now, at the ripe old age of sixty-something, with some 17,500 episodes under its belt and nigh on five million listeners per episode, *The Archers* has become a worldwide broadcasting phenomenon.

For millions of listeners, *The Archers* is far more than a radio drama – for 15 minutes each day it's a whole way of life. It shows the extent of the show's popularity that much of the extended life of *The Archers* has been mapped out, catalogued and endlessly debated by enthusiastic fans.

For the diehard, there are plenty of ways to get a top-up on the daily fix. You can indulge your addiction in one of the many Internet chat rooms, peruse online maps, catch up on missed episodes, or listen to clips and interviews on YouTube. And like all successful brands there is plenty of merchandise to spend your hard-earned cash on – from archive CDs to calendars, keyrings and mugs emblazoned with the words 'Keep Calm and Listen to *The Archers*'.

There is a whole canon of literature on *The Archers*, including novels (prequels, sequels and extended character stories), who's who guides, a range of cookbooks (the first published in 1977), and an encyclopaedia.

In 2011, an issue of the fictitious *Borsetshire Life: The County Magazine* contained a profile of the village of Ambridge and an interview with Alan Titchmarsh, who knows 'Ambridge' well, having appeared on the show in 2003 to judge a garden competition.

Spin-off *Archers* shows have been broadcast on television (such as the episode penned by Victoria Wood for Comic Relief in 2005, featuring *Archers* fans Stephen Fry, Ewan McGregor, Ian McKellen and Liza Tarbuck) and in the theatre. And if, as a real diehard fan, all that wasn't enough to feed your addiction, you could always attend the annual *Archers* convention, which has been held since 1994.

At the end of the day, perhaps the great strength of *The Archers*, and the secret to its enduring popularity, is that it brings us together as a nation and gives us a chance to show that we have a lighter side. But that is not to say that *Archers* fans are somehow being ironic in their loyalty to the show – far from it. There may be some who are not deadly serious, but for many that 7 p.m. slot is sacrosanct, Ambridge, Borchester and Felpersham are real places, and woe betide anyone who comes between them and their chance to catch up with events there.

A LITTLE 4 THOUGHT

The Archers is the longest-running soap opera in any format, anywhere in the world.

THAT THEME TUNE

Written in 1924 by the composer Arthur Wood, the theme tune 'Barwick Green' is a maypole dance from the suite *My Native Heath*. Billy Connolly once suggested that it should replace the National Anthem – and there are many who would agree with him. On April Fool's Day in 2004, the *Today* programme aired a new, up-to-date remix of the theme by Brian Eno, intended to 'increase the appeal to a younger audience'.

A LITTLE 4 THOUGHT

Ambridge is generally thought to be modelled on the village of Inkberrow in Worcestershire, although the residents of Rippingale in Lincolnshire also claim it as their own.

THE CHARACTERS

There are currently 128 characters in *The Archers*, including seventeen silent characters. Many of them belong to dynasties which have been a feature of the programme for literally generations. At the time of writing, the eponymous Archers account for fourteen of the characters, there are twelve Grundys, seven Tuckers, five Horrobins, four Aldridges and four Carters.

A LITTLE **4** THOUGHT

In real life Brian Aldridge (Charles Collingwood) and Shula Hebden Lloyd (Judy Bennett) are married.

In the mid 1990s Charles Collingwood played the eccentric scorekeeper on Noel Edmonds' BBC One quiz show *Telly Addicts*.

WEATHERING THE STORMS AT AMBRIDGE

Any soap opera location worth its salt has an unusually high incidence of drama. (For example, an average of twenty-one people a year are murdered in the picturesque county of Midsomer – many times higher than the national average.) And for sixty years, the folk of Ambridge have weathered more than their fair share of storms. Aside from higher-than-average rates of birth, death, marriage and divorce, dramas at Ambridge and the surrounding area include:

Racism (Roy Tucker in 1995, when he was part of a gang that threw acid in Usha's face)

Suicide (Greg Turner in 2004)

Cancer (Ruth Archer in 2000, Siobhan Donovan in 2007)

Infidelity (Lilian Bellamy in 2012, Brian Aldridge, recurring)

Homophobia (Sid Perks, towards Sean Myerson and Ian Craig)

Gambling (Alistair Lloyd, recurring)

Eating disorder (Helen Archer, following Greg's death)

Accidental death (Nigel Pargetter's fall in 2011)

... and even an armed siege at the village shop (Clive Horrobin in 2011)

A LITTLE  THOUGHT

In 2013 Graham Seed, who played the ill-fated Nigel Pargetter, returned to Radio 4 to play in a drama based on Dostoevsky's *The Gambler*. He said he had missed radio, and had 'tried very hard not to sound like Nigel Pargetter'.

LIFE ON THE FARM

Of course the various farms also experience the ups and downs of farming life. Between them over the years, the farms of Borsetshire – Bridge, Home, Grange, Nightingale, Willow and Brookfield – have been through foot and mouth, the vagaries of the weather, crop price fluctuations and an E. coli outbreak. They have also had their fair share of raging controversies – factory farming, GM versus organic, and the welfare of turkeys at Christmas.

FAMOUS FACES IN AMBRIDGE

Archers audiobooks have been narrated by famous names including Miriam Margolyes, Stella Gonet and Stephanie Cole, while making a cameo appearance seems to be de rigueur in A-list circles these days – but in fact it's nothing new. Celebs who've put in an appearance include:

Bradley Wiggins featured as himself in 2014, when he turned up at the Sport Relief Rough and Tumble Challenge. He witnessed a fight between Ian and Rob over Helen, and caused Lynda Snell to lose control of her cycle.

The Duchess of Cornwall appeared in 2011, to mark the 25th anniversary of the National Osteoporosis Society.

Crime novelist Colin Dexter made a cameo in 2010.

Robert Winston appeared as a fertility specialist consulted by Hayley and Roy Tucker in 2007.

Cricketer Mike Gatting appeared as himself in 2007.

Zandra Rhodes played herself in an episode in 2006 in connection with a charity fashion show.

DJ Chris Moyles appeared in 2004 as a customer in The Bull. He was suspected of being a National Pub of the Year judge.

Griff Rhys Jones appeared as himself in 2004, when Lynda Snell recruited him to her campaign to reopen The Cat and Fiddle pub.

In 2003 Alan Titchmarsh judged Ambridge's entries in the National Gardens Scheme open gardens competition.

Radio DJ John Peel appeared as himself in 1991.

Dame Judi Dench made an appearance in 1989 for the 10,000th episode. Terry Wogan was featured and Esther Rantzen was responsible for the sound effects.

Princess Margaret and the Duke of Westminster appeared in 1984 to mark the centenary of the NSPCC.

Others who have made appearances include Britt Ekland, Humphrey Lyttelton, Anneka Rice, Dame Edna Everage and Antony Gormley.

STOP PRESS: Kirstie Allsopp appeared in The Archers on 27 July to open the village fete, and she also lent her support to the Save Am Vale Environment campaign by posing in a SAVE t-shirt.

Portrait of a Pargetter As a Listener
ALISON DOWLING
Elizabeth Pargetter

My first memory of BBC Radio was... in Malta. I was born there, my grandfather was posted there whilst in the British Navy. My British mother married my Maltese father and they used to listen to the BBC World Service. It sounded like a symphony of crackles and noise interference as reception was so poor but it is a sound synonymous with my early childhood there.

When I'm not working I'm listening to... *Desert Island Discs*, *PM* and of course *The Archers*!

Radio 4 matters because... It pays my mortgage! ... and both educates and entertains. I would hate to be without it, my radio is like a best friend.

A LITTLE 4 THOUGHT

You can follow Sid Perks' ghost on Twitter, along with Sabrina Thwaite, Bartleby the Pony, Captain the Dog and the Ambridge Mice.

---

66 *The Archers is an anchor in a storm, always there no matter what you're going through. Key moments? Well, Lynda Snell's Christmas shows have got to be up there. Or when Lilian, playing the Wicked Queen in Snow White, set fire to one of the dwarves whilst having a crafty fag behind the magic mirror.* 99

ANNIE DAVIES, JOURNALIST

COMEDY AND LIGHT ENTERTAINMENT

The 6.30 p.m. comedy slot was created as part of James Boyle's 1998 shake-up of the Radio 4 schedule. These days, for many people it is a sacred half-hour, particularly on Mondays and Fridays when some of the most popular comedies are broadcast.

Radio 4's comedy output includes pretty much the whole range of formats. To name but a few that are current and/or recent:

Sketch shows: *Armstrong and Miller, Little Britain*

Panel games and quizzes: *Heresy, I'm Sorry I Haven't a Clue, Just a Minute, The News Quiz, The Unbelievable Truth*

Sitcoms: *Cabin Pressure, Clare in the Community, Count Arthur Strong, Ed Reardon's Week, Fags Mags and Bags, Rudy's Rare Records*

Stand-up/monologue: *Jeremy Hardy Speaks to the Nation, Mark Steel's in Town, Mark Thomas: The Manifesto, The Now Show* (@BBCNowShow)

Chat: *I've Never Seen Star Wars, My Teenage Diary, Chain Reaction*

HOME FOR A LAUGH?

In the early days comedy programmes tended to be aired on the Light Programme, then repeated on the Home Service. For example, *Beyond Our Ken* was broadcast on the Light Programme, and repeated on the Home Service at a later date. *Round the Horne* and *The Navy Lark* went out on the Light Programme, with repeats within the week. *Much-Binding-in-the-Marsh* was on the Light Programme, originally as part of *Merry Go Round* and then under its own title, but after several series and a name change, it reverted back to *Much-Binding* and ended up on the Home Service.*

COMEDY SURVIVORS

It's been said that comedy doesn't travel well and doesn't have a long shelf life – something which certainly seems to be true of comedy that relies on wit and satire. Though we laugh today at *The News Quiz* and *The Now Show*, it has to be said that future generations probably just won't get the humour.

The exception to this rule would appear to be comedy built on absurdity and a sense of the ridiculous – as long, that is, as it is irredeemably absurd. Here are some of the survivors:

THE GOON SHOW

It was in 1951 that the Goons – with the original line-up of Spike Milligan, Peter Sellers, Harry Secombe and Michael Bentine – first burst onto the airwaves, bringing with them some of the most absurd storylines, ludicrous characters, compelling catchphrases, indecipherable accents and fruity sound effects ever heard on radio.

---

* Thanks to Steve at the *Radio Times* Archive for clarification.

Bentine left after the second series to pursue his own career, and it was during the third series that Milligan suffered his first nervous breakdown, causing him to miss twelve programmes. But in spite of the hiccups, the show survived for over two hundred programmes and ten series.

When Milligan announced that he would be leaving at the end of the ninth series there was protest, pleading and a petition signed by 1,030 fans. The Goons recorded a tenth series, before finally signing off with the words: 'It's better to go out on top.'

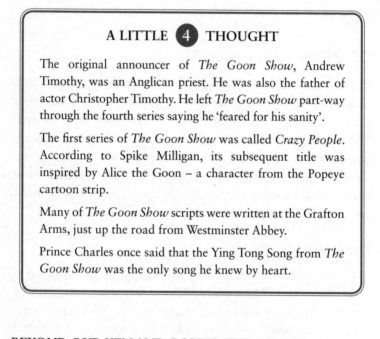

A LITTLE 4 THOUGHT

The original announcer of *The Goon Show*, Andrew Timothy, was an Anglican priest. He was also the father of actor Christopher Timothy. He left *The Goon Show* part-way through the fourth series saying he 'feared for his sanity'.

The first series of *The Goon Show* was called *Crazy People*. According to Spike Milligan, its subsequent title was inspired by Alice the Goon – a character from the Popeye cartoon strip.

Many of *The Goon Show* scripts were written at the Grafton Arms, just up the road from Westminster Abbey.

Prince Charles once said that the Ying Tong Song from *The Goon Show* was the only song he knew by heart.

BEYOND OUR KEN AND ROUND THE HORNE

Beyond Our Ken ran on the Light Programme between 1958 and 1964, and was the predecessor of *Round the Horne*, which ran from 1965 to 1968.

Both starred Kenneth Horne, Kenneth Williams, Hugh Paddick, Betty Marsden and Bill Pertwee, with Douglas Smith as the announcer, while *Round the Horne* also featured Marty Feldman and Barry Took.

Many of the innuendo-filled sketches in *Round the Horne* featured camp comedy duo Julian and Sandy (Paddick and Williams respectively). Although they were gay parodies, their mere inclusion in the programme in an era when homosexuality was illegal was risqué.

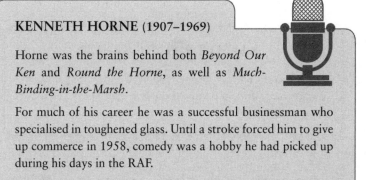

KENNETH HORNE (1907–1969)

Horne was the brains behind both *Beyond Our Ken* and *Round the Horne*, as well as *Much-Binding-in-the-Marsh*.

For much of his career he was a successful businessman who specialised in toughened glass. Until a stroke forced him to give up commerce in 1958, comedy was a hobby he had picked up during his days in the RAF.

Horne suffered a fatal heart attack in 1969, while hosting the annual Guild of Television Producers and Directors Awards.

A LITTLE **4** THOUGHT

A 1950 Pathé newsreel shows Kenneth Horne attempting a mocked-up smash-and-grab on an off-licence – only to be foiled by the toughened glass in the window. The voiceover announces: 'It looks as if 'Much-Binding' is the right phrase.'

I'M SORRY I'LL READ THAT AGAIN

This riotous show featured Tim Brooke-Taylor, John Cleese, Graeme Garden, David Hatch, Jo Kendall and Bill Oddie.

ISIRTA characters included: the Director General of the BBC (played by Cleese), American Continuity Man (a parody of Hughie Green played by Oddie), Angus Prune (Oddie), Grimbling (a 'dirty old man' played by Oddie), Lady Constance de Coverlet (Brooke-Taylor), Mr Arnold Totteridge (Garden), John and Mary (Cleese and Kendall) and Masher Wilkins (a kind-hearted simpleton played by Cleese).

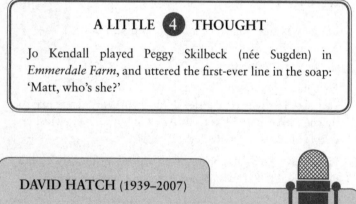

A LITTLE 4 THOUGHT

Jo Kendall played Peggy Skilbeck (née Sugden) in *Emmerdale Farm*, and uttered the first-ever line in the soap: 'Matt, who's she?'

DAVID HATCH (1939–2007)

The son of a clergyman, he joined the BBC in 1964, having been a shining light of the Cambridge Footlights at the same time as John Cleese.

A versatile man, Hatch was a writer, and one of the stars of *I'm Sorry I'll Read That Again*. He went on to become Controller of Radio 2 in 1980, Controller of Radio 4 in 1983 and Managing Director of BBC Network Radio in 1987.

THE NEWS QUIZ

PROGRAMME STATS

Running since: 1977

Current host: Sandi Toksvig (@sanditoksvig)

Past hosts: Barry Norman, Barry Took, Simon Hoggart

Description: Topical panel quiz show, taking its questions from the week's news stories.

Website: www.bbc.co.uk/programmes/b006r9yq

Twitter: @TheNewsQuiz

Begun as a 'frippery' and intended for one show only, *The News Quiz* has now run for nigh on forty years and over sixty seasons – and shows no sign of slowing down.

Created by John Lloyd, the original concept was to pit Alan Coren, the then editor of *Punch*, against Richard Ingrams, who was editor of *Private Eye*, in a head-to-head quiz about the news.

From the outset, the formula has remained essentially unchanged. Regular panellists these days include Susan Calman, Andy Hamilton, Jeremy Hardy, Francesca Martinez and Francis Wheen, who provide the 90 minutes' worth of material which is recorded on a Friday and edited to 28 minutes for transmission that evening.

IN MEMORIAM
LINDA SMITH (1958–2006)

For a heady few years, Radio 4 listeners and producers just couldn't get enough of the girl from Erith in Kent ('It's not twinned with anywhere, but it does have a suicide pact with Dagenham').

She was a regular on *The News Quiz*, *Just a Minute* and *I'm Sorry I Haven't a Clue*, as well as making television appearances on *Have I Got News for You*, *Mock the Week*, *Countdown* and *QI*. In 2002 she was voted the 'Wittiest Living Person' by Radio 4 listeners.

Tragically, Smith was diagnosed with ovarian cancer in 2001, and succumbed to it in 2006. Though gone, she is immortalised in many listeners' memories, with lines such as: 'Don't knock ASBOs, it's the only qualification some of these kids will ever get.'

A LITTLE **4** THOUGHT

Having appeared on Radio 4's *Devout Sceptics* programme, Linda Smith was President of the British Humanist Association from 2004 until her death in 2006.

NEWS QUIZ NEWSPAPER CLIPPING

A young girl who was blown out to sea on a set of inflatable teeth was rescued by a man on an inflatable lobster. A coastguard spokesman commented, 'this sort of thing is all too common'.

The Times

66 *The News Quiz is a must-listen, though usually on a Saturday morning with the kids in the car, so I have to quickly turn down the volume or ask a question loudly when there are rude bits. Sandi Toksvig is brilliant, sometimes makes me snort out loud.* 99

GEORGINA VIGLIECCA, MUM OF TWO

JUST A MINUTE

PROGRAMME STATS

Running since: 1967

Description: Panel game in which the contestants are challenged to speak for one minute without hesitation, deviation or repetition on any subject that comes up on the cards.

Website: www.bbc.co.uk/programmes/b006s5dp

Without deviation or hesitation but, it has to be said, plenty of repetition, Nicholas Parsons holds the record for the longest unbroken chairmanship of a radio show – nigh on fifty years, in fact.

Comedy writer David Quantick has ascribed *Just a Minute*'s success to its 'insanely basic' format, which allows a wide range of comedians to adapt their style to it.

The idea came to producer Ian Messiter who, as a schoolboy daydreaming in class, was suddenly brought back to reality by the booming voice of the teacher: 'Messiter! Repeat what I have been saying for the last minute, without hesitation or repetition.'

Nicholas Parsons was not originally slated as the chairman of *Just a Minute*. It came about because he hosted the pilot, which didn't go down well with the commissioning editors, although they did like the chairman – so he took it on as a challenge.

In the early years the likes of Clement Freud, Peter Jones, Derek Nimmo and Kenneth Williams were the 'staples' of the panel. In more than nine hundred shows, over two hundred panellists have taken part, among them Henry Blofeld, Barbara Castle, Fenella Fielding, Brian Johnston, Beryl Reid and Millie Small (famous for singing 'My Boy Lollipop').

They have spoken on subjects as diverse as: excuses for being late, keeping fit, phrenology, the English nanny, things to do in the bath, the many uses of bubble gum, and so on.

NUMBER OF APPEARANCES ON *JUST A MINUTE*

895   Nicholas Parsons (since 1967)
548   Clement Freud (1967–2009)
346   Kenneth Williams (1968–1988)
332   Peter Jones (1971–2000)
330   Paul Merton (since 1989)
311   Derek Nimmo (1967–1999)
128   Tony Hawks (since 1992)
96   Sheila Hancock (since 1967)
93   Graham Norton (since 1994)
83   Gyles Brandreth (since 1982)
57   Jenny Eclair (since 1994)
54   Andrée Melly (1968–1976), Sue Perkins (since 2000)
52   Julian Clary (since 1997)

MINUTEERS (CONTESTANTS WHO'VE GONE A WHOLE MINUTE FROM START TO FINISH)

66   Kenneth Williams
30   Clement Freud
23   Derek Nimmo
22   Paul Merton
21   Peter Jones

11   Sue Perkins
9   Gyles Brandreth
6   Sheila Hancock, Graham Norton
5   Pam Ayres

Portrait of the Presenter As a Listener
NICHOLAS PARSONS
Presenter, *Just a Minute*

My first memory of the Home Service is... There wasn't a lot of radio then, but we had a radio at home and we would sit down as a family around it. I loved *Band Waggon* with Arthur Askey and Richard Murdoch, and *In Town Tonight* ('In town tonight it is none other than...') on a Saturday evening, the first chat show of its kind ever. It was followed by *Music Hall*, with Elsie and Doris Waters, Murgatroyd and Winterbottom, Suzette Tarri and Ronnie Ronalde, who used to whistle.

When I'm not working I listen to... I love radio – love listening to it and love performing on it. All my radios at home are tuned into Radio 4. I wake up to it and listen to the *Today* programme while I'm getting dressed and doing my exercises. When I appeared on *Desert Island Discs* the luxury I chose to take with me was a radio tuned into Radio 4.

Radio 4 matters because... you can keep yourself completely educated and informed through it. It sustains the whole culture, and it isn't subject to commercial demands.

THINGS YOU (PROBABLY) NEVER KNEW ABOUT RADIO 4 6.30 p.m. COMEDY AND ITS PRESENTERS

Questions that have been debated on *Heresy* include: Are women better than men at expressing their emotions? Should public figures be allowed to have a private life? Is there something inherently naff about being middle class? Are we on the brink of an environmental catastrophe?

In 2009 Steve Punt and Hugh Dennis got into hot water on *The Now Show*, for referring to Michael Jackson and the IRA as both 'eighties celebrities'.

Sandi Toksvig made her first radio appearance on *Loose Ends*. After she did a report on a 'heavy leather' show from Earls Court, Ned Sherrin nicknamed her 'Studs Toksvig'.

Nicholas Parsons has appeared on every single show of *Just a Minute*, either as chairman or (occasionally) as a panellist.

Charles Collingwood's first appearance on *Just A Minute* was broadcast from the 2001 Edinburgh Festival. *Just A Minute* has broadcast a special show recorded at the Festival since 1993.

A LITTLE 4 THOUGHT

In 2001 the unlikely comedy pairing of Bob Monkhouse and Suggs joined forces in a sitcom *I Think I've Got a Problem*, about a man who wakes up one morning to discover that he can't stop singing at inappropriate moments.

FROM RADIO TO TELEVSION

A number of well-known television comedies started life in audio form on Radio 4. They include: *The [Mighty] Boosh, Dead Ringers, Little Britain, That Mitchell and Webb Sound, Goodness Gracious Me, Knowing Me, Knowing You, The Day Today, Whose Line Is It Anyway?* and *Room 101*.

THE BOOSH/THE MIGHTY BOOSH

In 2000, one of *The Mighty Boosh*'s three stage shows caught the attention of BBC producers at the Edinburgh Fringe, which led to *The Boosh* being broadcast in 2001 on BBC London Live. It later transferred to Radio 4, from where the television series developed.

ON THE TOWN/THE LEAGUE OF GENTLEMEN

On the Town was *The League of Gentlemen*'s radio forerunner. Just six episodes were broadcast, starting on 6 November 1997.

The town of Spent (*On the Town*) is Royston Vasey (*The League of Gentlemen*) in all but name. There were a few residents who didn't make the move, but not many, while a few people cropped up in the television series who hadn't existed on radio.

It was on Radio 4 that we were first introduced to Val and Harvey Denton (Mark Gatiss and Steve Pemberton) and the nephew who came to stay with them, Benjamin (Reece Shearsmith). And to Ross Gaines (Shearsmith), the intelligent one in Pauline Campbell-Jones's (Pemberton's) Job Centre Restart group, and Mickey M. Michaels (Gatiss), the not-so-intelligent one.

A LITTLE 4 THOUGHT

Whose Line Is It Anyway? is the one that got away, transferring from Radio 4 to Channel 4, where it became a hit. After that, BBC Radio and BBC Television agreed to keep successful formats in house.

Sitcoms which have been adapted for Radio 4 having been successful on television include: *Dad's Army*, *Whatever Happened to the Likely Lads?*, *Yes Minister* and *As Time Goes By*.

QUIZZES

BRAIN OF BRITAIN

PROGRAMME STATS

Running since: 1953

Current host: Russell Davies (since 2009)

Past hosts: Franklin Engelmann (until 1972), Robert Robinson (1972–2008), Peter Snow (2007)

Description: The nationwide general knowledge contest in which forty-eight listeners from all parts of the United Kingdom fight their way to the final. The prize is a silver salver and the title, Brain of Britain.

Website: www.bbc.co.uk/programmes/b00813s0

The longest-running of all broadcast quiz shows began as a slot in *What Do You Know?*, before becoming a programme in its own right in 1967. It was chaired by Franklin Engelmann until his death in 1972.

Brain of Britain was hosted by Robert Robinson for most of its life, although during his illness the 2004 series was hosted by Russell Davies.

Peter Snow took over the role briefly in 2007, also due to the illness of Robinson, dispensing with Robinson's trademark style of addressing contestants by their honorific and surname (e.g. 'Mr Smith').

IN MEMORIAM
ROBERT ROBINSON (1927–2011)

It seems it was all too easy to lampoon Robert Robinson – a token of affection, of course, but one that you can imagine became wearing at times:

Private Eye nicknamed him 'Smuggins'.

In *Not the Nine O'Clock News* an actor portrayed him wearing a cricket box over his forehead.

In *A Bit of Fry and Laurie*, Stephen Fry and Hugh Laurie both impersonated him presenting a spoof programme 'The Smug Hour'.

The presenter of spoof game show 'Numberwang' in *That Mitchell and Webb Look* is based on Robinson.

He appeared in a *Viz* comic strip as Robin Robertson.

A LITTLE 4 THOUGHT

Controversy surrounded *Brain of Britain* in 2013, when 'professional quizzer' Barry Simmons made it to the final. Simmons had appeared in numerous quiz shows, including the BBC series *Eggheads*, for which he was paid. He had also won £64,000 in *Who Wants to Be a Millionaire?*

I'M SORRY I HAVEN'T A CLUE

PROGRAMME STATS

Running since: 1972

Current presenter: Jack Dee (@TheRealJackDee)

Past presenter: Humphrey Lyttelton ('Humph') (1972–2008)

Regular panellists: Tim Brooke-Taylor, Barry Cryer, Graeme Garden

Past panellists: John Cleese (1972), Bill Oddie (1972–1974), Jo Kendall (1972), Willie Rushton (1974–1996)

Guest panellists: Bill Bailey, Max Boyce, Jo Brand, Marcus Brigstocke, Rob Brydon, Susan Calman, Denise Coffey, Kenny Everett, John Finnemore, Stephen Fry, Andy Hamilton, Mike Harding, Jeremy Hardy, Tony Hawks, Harry Hill, John Junkin, Phill Jupitus, Miles Jupp, Jonathan Lynn, Fred MacAulay, Paul Merton, David Mitchell, Neil Mullarkey, Ross Noble, Sue Perkins, Linda Smith, Bill Tidy, Sandi Toksvig, Victoria Wood

Guest appearance: Raymond Baxter (to commentate on Mornington Crescent sessions)

At the piano: Colin Sell (since 1974); occasional guest appearances by Neil Innes

Listening figures: Around 2.5 million

Description: The antidote to panel games.

Website: www.isihac.net/index.php

Twitter: (@ISIHAClue)

The phenomenon that is *I'm Sorry I Haven't a Clue* (*ISIHAC*) was originally devised as a non-scripted alternative to *I'm Sorry I'll Read That Again*.

In 1974 Bill Oddie was replaced on *ISIHAC* by Willie Rushton, and from thereon until 1996, the panel consisted of Rushton alongside Barry Cryer, Graeme Garden and Tim Brooke-Taylor, with Humphrey Lyttelton in the chair.

Samantha came on board to score the team's points in 1985, and Mrs Trellis from North Wales started writing to the show in 1990. She has been a regular, if befuddled, correspondent ever since.

Since Rushton's death in 1996 following heart surgery, the fourth seat on the panel has been occupied by a variety of guests.

In April 2008, 'Humph' and the team were booked to appear in the stage version of the programme in Bournemouth. It was announced that he was unwell, and his place was taken by Rob Brydon. A message from Humph was played to the audience: 'I'm sorry I can't be with you today as I am in hospital – I wish I'd thought of this sooner!'

JUST A FEW OF THE SILLY THINGS THE PANEL ARE GIVEN TO DO

Cheddar Gorge
Just a Minim
Late Arrivals
Letter Writing
Mornington Crescent
One Song to the Tune of Another
Pick-up Song
Quote … Misquote
Sound Charades
Swanee Kazoo
Uxbridge English Dictionary

MORNINGTON CRESCENT

With each episode of *ISIHAC*, millions of listeners doggedly try to decipher the rules of this confoundingly impenetrable yet ingeniously simple game.

Mornington Crescent is such an institution that it has a whole infrastructure, with a number of associations and groups dedicated to it. *The Little Book of Mornington Crescent* lists just a few of these bodies: the All-England British Mornington Crescent Federation, the Royal Mornington Crescent Legion, and the Mornington Crescent Staff Social Club.

The Little Book of Mornington Crescent also informs us that the term 'Mornington Crescent' is actually a bastardisation. It reveals that Samuel Pepys' account of having the Lytteltons around for fish supper notes that they played 'the genteel game of Moaning Tom Cheshunt'. The origins of that, however, remain obscure, as all that is recorded after that is that the evening ended with a game of bottle-spinning.

In spite of the books that have been written about its origins and history, and the associations and individuals who dedicate their time to trying to decipher its meaning, it remains an elusive, baffling game that only an elite few will ever fully understand.

A LITTLE 4 THOUGHT

In 2013, tickets for a live recording of *ISIHAC* at the Theatre Royal, Drury Lane sold out in 5 minutes.

❝ If you've understood Mornington Crescent,
nothing else in your life makes sense. ❞
JEREMY HARDY

UXBRIDGE ENGLISH DICTIONARY

The chairman introduces this round by explaining that much has changed in recent years, particularly when it comes to the use of the English language. He then asks the teams to provide examples they've spotted of how words have changed their meaning over time.

Typical suggestions might include: 'Reincarnation – to be born again as a tin of condensed milk', and 'Lovelorn – to be really, really fond of grass'.

The all-time great example, in many people's estimation, came from Stephen Fry – and uttered with not a little venom: 'Countryside – to kill Piers Morgan'.

ONE SONG TO THE TUNE OF ANOTHER

As the chairman explains, a song is very much like a clothing-store mannequin: the clothes represent the words while the model represents the tune. Here are a few classics:

Barry Cryer sings the words of 'The Laughing Policeman' to the tune of 'As Time Goes By'.

Jeremy Hardy sings the words of 'I Tawt I Taw a Puddy Tat' to the tune of 'I Vow to Thee My Country'. (When he's finished, Humph sighs 'Never mind'.)

Rob Brydon sings 'Baby Got Back' by Sir Mix-a-Lot to the tune of Billy Joel's 'I Love You Just the Way You Are'.

Graeme Garden sings 'I'm Too Sexy' by Right Said Fred to the tune of 'Frère Jacques', with the other cast joining in rounds.

Victoria Wood sings 'Bob the Builder' to the tune of 'I Dreamed a Dream'.

David Mitchell sings 'A Whiter Shade of Pale' to the tune of *The Muppet Show*.

Linda Smith sings Talking Heads' 'Psycho Killer' to the tune of 'Save Your Love' by Renée and Renato.

Sandi Toksvig sings 'Ain't No Sunshine' by Bill Withers to the tune of 'God Rest Ye Merry Gentlemen'.

A LITTLE ④ THOUGHT

The pilot show was called *I'm Sorry, They're At It Again*. It featured Graeme Garden and Jo Kendall performing the lyrics of 'Three Blind Mice' to the tune of 'Ol' Man River', and Bill Oddie and Tim Brooke-Taylor singing 'Sing a Song of Sixpence' to 'These Foolish Things'.

LATE ARRIVALS

Illustrious guests at the ball include the likes of Mr and Mrs Roids and their daughter Emma Roids.

Inevitably, every ball is attended by representatives from the Bennett dynasty – a large family whose surname has been hyphenated many times to create numerous double- and triple-barrelled versions. An example would be Mr and Mrs Bennett-Thatstwicetheestimate, who attended the Builders' Ball. Something else to say about the Bennetts is that, though they are a large and diverse family, they always honour the tradition of naming their eldest son Gordon. In this case, of course, the announcement was Gordon Bennett-Thatstwicetheestimate.

If Gordons crop up regularly, a popular name for girls in these circles is Shirley. For example, Mr and Mrs That-Holeinthegroundcantbeatoilet attended the Frenchman's Ball with their daughter, Shirley That-Holeinthegroundcantbeatoilet. Attending the same event were Mr and Mrs Alouetta and their son Jonty, and Mr and Mrs Fembargo and their cousin British Bea Fembargo.

RUNNING GAGS

'Bring me the head of… '.

Hamish and Dougal ('You'll have had your tea… ').

Correspondence from Mrs Trellis of North Wales.

And of course the lovely Samantha.

'And so, ladies and gentlemen' … 'as the chill wind of time carries aloft the solitary snowflake of destiny, and Network SouthEast closes down for the week, I notice it's very nearly the end of the show. But there's just time… '

A LITTLE 4 THOUGHT

Barry Cryer shared the chairmanship with Humphrey Lyttelton during the first series.

The theme tune is called 'The Schickel Shamble', and comes from the film *Monte Carlo or Bust*.

The long-suffering Colin Sell never replies to the insults that are hurled his way from the chair – in fact he can't, because nobody's given him a microphone.

Samantha is said to be based on Page 3 Girl Samantha Fox.

Samantha has occasionally been replaced by stand-ins, including Sven from Sweden and the lovely Monica. In addition, shortly after Margaret Thatcher left office in 1990, Humph introduced a new scorer named Margaret.

IN MEMORIAM
HUMPHREY LYTTELTON (1921–2008)

From an early age he developed a love affair with the trumpet. His mother bought him his first at fifteen, when the two of them slipped out of a match at Lord's Cricket Ground to go shopping in the music shops on the Charing Cross Road.

His lifelong left-leaning views came from a time when he was dispatched, after leaving Eton, to a steel mill in South Wales to see if he was cut out as a 'captain of industry'. Evidently he was not.

He joined the Grenadier Guards in 1941. Two years later, as the story goes, he waded ashore during the Allied landings in southern Italy, brandishing a pistol in one hand and his trumpet in the other.

As well as a jazz musician and broadcaster, 'Humph' did stints as a cartoonist, a restaurant critic for *Vogue* and a columnist for *Punch*.

He presented the Radio 2 programme *The Best of Jazz* from 1968 until the year of his death – four years longer than his chairmanship of *ISIHAC*.

IN MEMORIAM
WILLIE RUSHTON (1937–1996)

Willie Rushton met Paul Foot and Richard Ingrams while they were pupils at Shrewsbury School, and together they created *The Wallopian*, a satirical version of their school magazine, *The Salopian*.

In 1961, he put together the first issue of *Private Eye* in his bedroom using Letraset, and created the cartoon character who still appears in the top left-hand corner of the cover.

In 1962/1963 he started appearing alongside David Frost in *That Was the Week That Was*, where he became famous for his impersonation of Prime Minister Harold Macmillan.

In 1963 he stood at the Perth and Kinross by-election against Alec Douglas-Home. Although he garnered only forty-five votes, he seized the opportunity to denounce the prime minister at a large public meeting, calling him 'completely arrogant'.

He took part in twenty-seven series of *I'm Sorry I Haven't a Clue* and, nearly two decades after his untimely death, he has not been permanently replaced. Instead a different guest takes the place he vacated on the panel.

As producer Jon Naismith put it: 'As befits such an irreplaceable character, he has never been formally replaced.'

ARTS, CULTURE AND HISTORY

THE ART OF MAKING RADIO

If you're into the arts, tune into Radio 4 and you can find artists, writers, musicians, critics and reviewers talking about sculpture, photography, fine art, film, theatre, television, literature in all its many forms, and music and its innumerable sub-genres. There is, surely, something for everybody, with the possible exception of the classical music buff, who must turn a few notches of the dial to Radio 3.

If you're a film buff, for example, there's *The Film Programme*. You might find Helen Mirren discussing how she played Hitchcock's wife Alma Reville (2013), or a revealing interview with Denzel Washington on playing an alcoholic in *Flight* (2013).

Some of the most compelling programming about the arts might not take the arts per se as its starting point, but might look at the subject through a specific lens, such as from a historical point of view. An example of this was Francine Stock's three-part series *The Cultural Front* in 2014, which looked at the impact of World War One on the arts, and vice versa. Among the programme's many fascinating insights was the fact that some of the 'grandees' of the British literary establishment – H. G. Wells, J. M. Barrie, John Galsworthy and Arthur Conan Doyle – were secretly convened as the British War Propaganda Bureau, to discuss ways in which they could influence public opinion.

KALEIDOSCOPE AND *FRONT ROW*

PROGRAMME STATS

Running since: 1973 (*Kaleidoscope*, until 1998), 1998 (*Front Row*)

Current presenters: John Wilson, Kirsty Lang (@bbckirstylang)

Past presenters: Mark Lawson (1998–2014), Francine Stock (@FrancineFilm)

Description: Live magazine programme on the worlds of arts, literature, film, media and music.

Website: www.bbc.co.uk/programmes/b006qsq5

Twitter: @BBCFrontRow

Kaleidoscope's presenters included influential critics and high-flyers from the arts world: the critic Michael Billington, playwright Ronald Harwood, former Channel 4 Head of Arts Waldemar Januszczak and arts writer and critic Sheridan Morley. It was scrapped in the 1998 shake-up of the Radio 4 schedules, to be replaced by *Front Row*.

Strangely, *Kaleidoscope*'s original remit was to cover both arts and science. As editor Rosemary Hart recalls, a programme in those days might include 'the new Van Gogh Museum in Amsterdam with research on aggressive anemones', or 'Chinese acrobats at the London Coliseum combined with a talk on painless dentistry'. This uneasy 'arranged marriage' lasted only a year before the union was dissolved, and the stand was given over to pure arts coverage.

SOME NOTABLE GUESTS WHO'VE APPEARED ON *KALEIDOSCOPE* OR *FRONT ROW*:

1973	Anthony Burgess
1975	Graham Greene
1978	Henry Moore
1989	Saul Bellow
1991	Francis Bacon (his last interview)
1994	Charlie Watts, Joseph Heller, Leonard Cohen
1995	Scott Walker
1997	Elton John, Paul McCartney
2000	Lou Reed
2010	P. D. James
2011	Meryl Streep

CULTURAL EXCHANGE

In 2013, Tracey Emin presented 'Cultural Exchange', a mini-series within *Front Row*, where seventy-five guests were invited to describe and discuss their favourite or most inspirational piece of art. In the first programme Emin herself chose Vermeer's painting *Lady Writing a Letter with her Maid*.

The range of guests chose from the whole spectrum of the arts, among them:

Mark Haddon (the Uffington White Horse)

Terry Jones (*Under Milk Wood*)

Adrian Lester ('Redemption Song' by Bob Marley)

Meera Syal (*To Kill a Mockingbird*)

Richard Rogers (Piazza del Campo in Siena)

Justin Welby, Archbishop of Canterbury (Benjamin Britten's *War Requiem*)

A LITTLE  THOUGHT

In 2010 actor Russell Crowe swore at *Front Row* presenter Mark Lawson before leaving the studio when he was asked if his Robin Hood accent had hints of Irish in it.

THINGS YOU (PROBABLY) NEVER KNEW ABOUT RADIO 4 ARTS PRESENTERS PAST AND PRESENT

When Waldemar Januszczak was *The Guardian*'s Art Critic, the Features Editor was Richard Gott, who has been heavily implicated as a 'KGB agent of influence'. Despite having accompanied Gott to Moscow on a 'writing and drinking assignment', Januszczak 'never suspected a thing'.

Born in Nigeria, Kirsty Lang's schooling took place in Tokyo, Melbourne, Devon and Geneva.

Sheridan Morley (1941–2007) was the son of actor Robert Morley, and numbered Joanna Lumley among his cousins.

Francine Stock met her husband, Robert Lance Hughes, when he gave her an 'absurdly low quote' for converting her loft in order to get to know her better.

John Wilson's father is former Arsenal goalkeeper Bob Wilson.

MUSIC

If you're a music fan you might have caught Joe Dunthorne's *Lessons from the Mosh Pit* on *Four Thought* (2012), or tuned into the 2008 documentary that followed the fortunes of celebrated Iraqi heavy metal band Acrassicauda, or accompanied Lenny

Henry on a musical road trip around South Africa in 2010. Then there was the programme about a 175-year-old cymbal that led into an investigation of the history of percussion (2009)... the list goes on.

EARLY MUSIC BROADCASTING

In the early days the question was not so much about types of music, more about the quality of recording music. The logistics of recording a concert in a vast space such as the Albert Hall are a challenge for any technician, so it's remarkable, really, to think how determined BBC Radio was to include music as part of its output.

1927   The Proms becomes the BBC Proms, and is broadcast for the first time from the Albert Hall.

1928   First broadcast of the BBC Dance Orchestra.

1930   First broadcast of the BBC Symphony Orchestra, conducted by Adrian Boult.

MY MUSIC

The long-running *My Music* ran for 520 episodes over twenty-seven years, between 1967 and 1994. Each panel consisted of two pairings of one comedian and one music buff (Ian Wallace and Denis Norden versus David Franklin/John Amis and Frank Muir), who went head-to-head to answer questions put to them by host Steve Race. Each show ended with a good old-fashioned music-hall-style sing-song.

started in 1957, and reveal that Warren Beatty was among those who tried out for a part in *West Side Story*. He didn't get the part, despite Bernstein describing him as 'charming as hell'.

A LITTLE **4** THOUGHT

As well as presenting *Tales from the Stave*, Frances Fyfield is a lawyer and crime writer, whose novels have been translated into fourteen languages and adapted for television.

WRITE ON

If literature is your thing, you can find out about the poetry of the American Civil War (2011), or listen to Anne Fine's personal defence of the much-maligned children's story writer Enid Blyton (2009).

Radio 4's literary output includes:

A Good Read – Each guest brings a book to discuss in a three-way discussion. Hosted by Harriett Gilbert.

Open Book – Mariella Frostrup talking to authors and publishers of both fiction and non-fiction.

Bookclub – Led by James Naughtie. A group of readers talk to acclaimed authors about their best-known works.

Quote... Unquote – A celebrity panel game about quotations.

From Fact to Fiction – A writer creates a fictional response to a story on the news.

The Write Stuff – Billed as 'the radio panel game of literary correctness', it has been running since 1988. Chaired by James Walton, with team captains John Walsh and Sebastian Faulks.

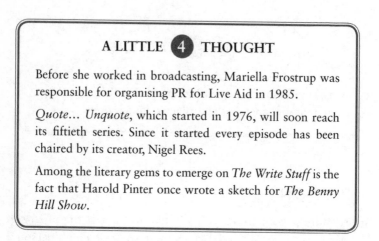

A LITTLE 4 THOUGHT

Before she worked in broadcasting, Mariella Frostrup was responsible for organising PR for Live Aid in 1985.

Quote... Unquote, which started in 1976, will soon reach its fiftieth series. Since it started every episode has been chaired by its creator, Nigel Rees.

Among the literary gems to emerge on *The Write Stuff* is the fact that Harold Pinter once wrote a sketch for *The Benny Hill Show*.

POETRY PLEASE

PROGRAMME STATS

Running since: 1979

Current presenter: Roger McGough

Past presenter: Frank Delaney

Description: A weekly selection of favourite poetry requested by listeners.

Website: www.bbc.co.uk/programmes/b006qp7q

In 2013, *The Guardian* published a list of the ten poems which featured most often on the programme:

'Stopping by Woods on a Snowy Evening', by Robert Frost

'How Do I Love Thee? Let Me Count the Ways',
by Elizabeth Barrett Browning

'Adlestrop', by Edward Thomas

'Fern Hill', by Dylan Thomas

'The Darkling Thrush', by Thomas Hardy

'Dover Beach', by Matthew Arnold

'Let Me Not to the Marriage of True Minds',
by William Shakespeare

'The Listeners', by Walter de la Mare

'Remember', by Christina Rossetti

'To His Coy Mistress', by Andrew Marvell

A LITTLE 4 THOUGHT

Poetry Please is the longest-running poetry request show on any station, anywhere in the world.

In 1995, a television viewers' poll found Rudyard Kipling's 'If' to be the nation's favourite poem.

In the 1960s Roger McGough, John Gorman and Mike McGear (Paul McCartney's brother) were in The Scaffold, the Liverpool band who had a number one hit with 'Lily the Pink'.

The voices of *Poetry Please* have included many of the nation's great actors: among them Judi Dench, Ian McKellen, Prunella Scales and Timothy West.

66 *[Poetry Please is] a kind of cardiogram of the country written through its poetry.* 99

PRODUCER TIM DEE IN *THE GUARDIAN*, SEPTEMBER 2013

66 *'Poetry *Click*' as the radio is switched off. I think that was one of Jack Dee's lines from the ever-wonderful* I'm Sorry I Haven't a Clue. 99

DAVE HUGHES, PLANNING OFFICER

MY OWN SHAKESPEARE

Vultures who like their culture a bit more highbrow might have tuned into *My Own Shakespeare* in 2012 – a ten-part series in which public figures were asked the simple question: 'Which piece of Shakespeare would you save from a burning building?' Their choices were read by well-known actors, and included:

Andrew Marr and Gyles Brandreth both chose a speech from *King Lear* (Act 5 Scene 3) when Lear has gone mad. The reader was David Warner.

Lawyer Shami Chakrabarti chose Isabella's speech from *Measure for Measure* (Act 2 Scene 2). It was read by Hattie Morahan.

Actor Don Warrington read Ulysses' speech from Act 3 Scene 3 of *Troilus and Cressida*. It was the choice of politician Michael Portillo, who chose it because he said it is about politics, government, and 'how to run a war'.

THE REITH LECTURES (@BBC_REITH)

On 26 December 1948 John Reith listened to the first of the lectures which still bear his name. After hearing Bertrand

Russell's lecture, he recorded in his diary: 'He went too far too quickly and has a bad voice anyhow... However, I wrote him a civil note...'

Between 1948 and 2013, seventy people delivered over 360 lectures. Until 1989, each lecturer was invited to deliver six talks, although since then the number has varied between five or six lectures.

In over fifty-five years, the Reith Lectures have built a reputation for being ahead of the debate. In 1952, for example, historian Arnold Toynbee was one of a very few people discussing the impact of westernisation in Muslim countries. While in 1969 the ecologist Frank Fraser Darling delivered a series titled 'Wilderness and Plenty', in which he warned of the onset of global warming. It was not at the time a subject taken particularly seriously.

In his 1962 lecture series entitled 'This Island Now', anthropologist George Carstairs caused consternation with his ideas about teenage sex. In the third lecture, 'The Vicissitudes of Teenagers', he introduced the subject in his clipped Edinburgh accent, questioning whether chastity is 'the supreme moral virtue'. Taking the example of Samoan culture, he concluded that 'many societies get on quite well without premarital chastity'.

Though prestigious, delivering the Reith Lectures inevitably puts the lecturer in a spotlight – not always a comfortable position to be in. In 1978 Edward Norman presented six lectures in a series called 'Christianity and the World', in which he argued that Christianity had become disastrously secularised and politicised. Many years later he told the BBC that his controversial lectures had hindered his career, saying it was 'the price you pay for seeking ideas which are true'.

On a couple of occasions the series of lectures has been divvied up between two or more lecturers. In 2000, to mark the new millennium, the Reith Lectures were delivered by five different thinkers on the subject of sustainable development. The final lecture consisted of a round-table discussion between all five lecturers and the Prince of Wales. In 2011 Aung San Suu Kyi and Eliza Manningham-Buller shared the platform to deliver lectures on the subject of 'Securing Freedom'.

That same year (2011), to celebrate sixty years of the Reith Lectures, the BBC published an archive containing sixty years of audio archive and transcripts. The collection is nearly, but not quite, complete, and the BBC has appealed for copies of the missing recordings.

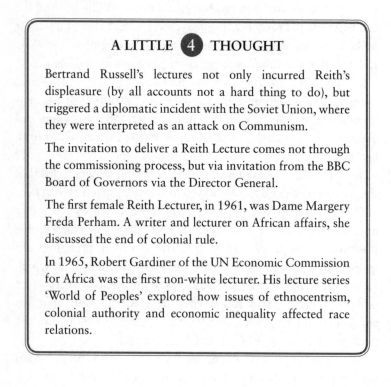

A LITTLE 4 THOUGHT

Bertrand Russell's lectures not only incurred Reith's displeasure (by all accounts not a hard thing to do), but triggered a diplomatic incident with the Soviet Union, where they were interpreted as an attack on Communism.

The invitation to deliver a Reith Lecture comes not through the commissioning process, but via invitation from the BBC Board of Governors via the Director General.

The first female Reith Lecturer, in 1961, was Dame Margery Freda Perham. A writer and lecturer on African affairs, she discussed the end of colonial rule.

In 1965, Robert Gardiner of the UN Economic Commission for Africa was the first non-white lecturer. His lecture series 'World of Peoples' explored how issues of ethnocentrism, colonial authority and economic inequality affected race relations.

REITH LECTURES

1948 Bertrand Russell 'Authority and the Individual'

1949 Robert Birley 'Britain in Europe'

1950 John Zachary Young 'Doubt and Certainty in Science'

1951 Lord Radcliffe 'Power and the State'

1952 Arnold J. Toynbee 'The World and the West'

1953 Robert Oppenheimer 'Science and the Common Understanding'

1954 Oliver Franks 'Britain and the Tide of World Affairs'

1955 Nikolaus Pevsner 'The Englishness of English Art'

1956 Edward Appleton 'Science and the Nation'

1957 George F. Kennan 'Russia, the Atom and the West'

1958 Bernard Lovell 'The Individual and the Universe'

1959 Peter Medawar 'The Future of Man'

1960 Edgar Wind 'Art and Anarchy'

1961 Margery Perham 'The Colonial Reckoning'

1962 George Carstairs 'This Island Now'

1963 Albert Sloman 'A University in the Making'

1964 Leon Bagrit 'The Age of Automation'

1965 Robert Gardiner 'World of Peoples'

1966 John K. Galbraith 'The New Industrial State'

1967 Edmund Leach 'A Runaway World'

1968 Lester Pearson 'Peace in the Family of Man'

1969 Frank Fraser Darling 'Wilderness and Plenty'

1970 Donald Schön 'Change and Industrial Society'

1971 Richard Hoggart 'Only Connect'

1972 Andrew Shonfield 'Europe: Journey to an Unknown Destination'

1973 Alistair Buchan 'Change Without War'

1974   Ralf Dahrendorf 'The New Liberty'

1975   Daniel Boorstin 'America and the World Experience'

1976   Colin Blakemore 'Mechanics of the Mind'

1977   A. H. Halsey 'Change in British Society'

1978   Edward Norman 'Christianity and the World'

1979   Ali Mazrui 'The African Condition'

1980   Ian Kennedy 'Unmasking Medicine'

1981   Laurence Martin 'The Two-Edged Sword'

1982   Denis Donoghue 'The Arts without Mystery'

1983   Douglas Wass 'Government and the Governed'

1984   John Searle 'Minds, Brains and Science'

1985   David Henderson 'Innocence and Design'

1986   John McCluskey 'Law, Justice and Democracy'

1987   Alexander Goehr 'The Survival of the Symphony'

1988   Geoffrey Hosking 'The Rediscovery of Politics'

1989   Jacques Darras 'Beyond the Tunnel of History'

1990   Jonathan Sacks 'The Persistence of Faith'

1991   Steve Jones 'The Language of the Genes'

1992   No lecture broadcast

1993   Edward Said 'Representation of the Intellectual'

1994   Marina Warner 'Managing Monsters'

1995   Richard Rogers 'Sustainable City'

1996   Jean Aitchison 'The Language Web'

1997   Patricia Williams 'The Genealogy of Race'

1998   John Keegan 'War in Our World'

1999   Anthony Giddens 'Runaway World'

2000   Chris Patten, John Browne, Thomas Lovejoy, Gro Harlem Brundtland, Vandana Shiva & Charles, Prince of Wales 'Respect for the Earth'

2001   Tom Kirkwood 'The End of Age'

2002   Onora O'Neill 'A Question of Trust'

2003   Vilayanur S. Ramachandran 'The Emerging Mind'

2004   Wole Soyinka 'Climate of Fear'

2005   Alec Broers 'The Triumph of Technology'

2006   Daniel Barenboim 'In the Beginning was Sound'

2007   Jeffrey Sachs 'Bursting at the Seams'

2008   Jonathan Spence 'Chinese Vistas'

2009   Michael Sandel 'A New Citizenship'

2010   Martin Rees 'Scientific Horizons'

2011   Aung San Suu Kyi & Eliza Manningham-Buller 'Securing Freedom'

2012   Niall Ferguson 'The Rule of Law and Its Enemies'

2013   Grayson Perry 'Playing to the Gallery'

GRAYSON PERRY – 2013 REITH LECTURER

In 2013, amid a glare of publicity, Turner Prize winner Grayson Perry was invited to present the BBC Reith Lecture. In a series titled 'Playing to the Gallery', Perry discussed what he said was a 'burning issue'– 'How do we tell if something is good?'

In his first talk, 'Democracy Has Bad Taste', he explored the idea that the most popular art isn't necessarily the best. Among his insights were the theory that 'You'll never have a good art career unless your work fits into the elevator of a New York apartment block', and the idea that red paintings will always sell best, followed by white, blue, yellow, green and black. He also shared the fact that his first bad review had opened with the words: 'If I had a hammer…'

HISTORY

History is one of those subjects that crops up in many guises on Radio 4 – a documentary, for example, about the history of disability (*Disability: A New History*, presented by Peter White in 2012), or mathematics (*A Brief History of Mathematics*, presented by Marcus du Sautoy in 2014), or kissing (*A Kiss Is... Never Just a Kiss*, presented by Rowan Pelling in 2012) or Shakespeare's Globe Theatre (*A Very Theatrical Revolution*, presented by Dominic Dromgoole in 2009).

It is here, at the intersection of two subjects, that history is applied to life, and once again rouses the curiosity of the Radio 4 listener. Another example is the *Document* strand, which took a look again at significant events from history (the Hyderabad Massacre, Pearl Harbour, Votes for Women), taking a single document as its starting point.

ARCHIVE ON 4

PROGRAMME STATS

Description: A look back at programmes and recordings from the BBC archives.

Website: www.bbc.co.uk/programmes/b00hg8dq

The show described by Nosheen Iqbal of *The Guardian* as 'classy... clever, witty, erudite... this dreamboat documentary strand is the perfect first date of radio'.

For example, the episode titled *The First Generation X* is a fascinating insight into the teenagers who, in the 1960s, 'seemed to embody a new sense of rebellion'. The programme also unearthed a rare excerpt from *The Under 20 Club*, a programme broadcast for adolescents on the Home Service in the late 1930s, a time when young people were also perceived to be a problem.

THIS SCEPTRED ISLE

When Radio 4 does 'pure' history, it is often a landmark series such as *This Sceptred Isle* (from 1995). It took the form of 216 fifteen-minute segments broadcast twice a day – a total of 46 hours. It was narrated by Anna Massey with Paul Eddington reading extracts from documents. Sadly, Eddington died during the production, and his role was taken on by Peter Jeffrey.

In 1999, Radio 4 extended the programme to cover the twentieth century from 1901 (where the original series had ended) to the end of the millennium. It was broadcast between August and December. Again, Anna Massey was the narrator, with Robert Powell providing the readings.

In 2001 another shorter series, *This Sceptred Isle: Dynasties*, was produced. It told the stories of the powerful and influential families of Britain and Ireland, such as the Churchills.

Then again, in 2005 and 2006, *This Sceptred Isle: Empire* was a ninety-part history of the British Empire. This time the narrator was Juliet Stevenson, alongside a cast of readers including Joss Ackland, Christopher Eccleston and Anna Massey.

DAY BY DAY

Every day for six months in 2008, Radio 4 broadcast *Day By Day 1968*, a season of programmes to mark the fortieth anniversary of 'a momentous year'.

The idea was revived in 2014 to mark the centenary of World War One.

A HISTORY OF THE WORLD IN 100 OBJECTS

A hundred-part landmark series broadcast in 2010, *A History of the World in 100 Objects* was transmitted in fifteen-minute programmes over twenty weeks.

It was a joint project between Radio 4 and the British Museum, and was written and presented by the museum's director Neil MacGregor.

The hundred objects included a statue of a Maya maize god, the Ancient Egyptian Rosetta Stone, a seventeenth-century German broadsheet commemorating the Reformation, a Japanese print of a wave, a penny defaced by a suffragette, and a credit card.

Each object told a story that in turn illuminated a period of history. A silver plate, for example, showing a king slaying a deer, led into the story of the Sasanians, the first Iranian dynasty to promote Zoroastrianism as the state religion.

Another object was a Victorian Wedgwood tea set – symbolic of the technological innovation which led to the mass production of goods, making luxuries like tea and Wedgwood pottery affordable to working-class people for the first time.

Additional contributions came from people as diverse as David Attenborough, Bob Geldof, Madhur Jaffrey, Jonathan Sacks and Rowan Williams.

The project has inspired similar projects in museums around the world, as well as an ambitious web-based project, where people can submit their own objects.

A LITTLE 4 THOUGHT

Neil MacGregor's master's degree was supervised by Anthony Blunt, later exposed as a Soviet spy. Blunt later said that he considered MacGregor the most brilliant pupil he ever taught.

PERSONAL HISTORY

Many of the programmes that are termed 'life stories' on Radio 4 fall at the intersection of history and culture. They include the obituary programme *Last Word*, presented by Matthew Bannister, or the tribute programme *Great Lives*, fronted by Matthew Parris. Each programme is in effect a mini history of a particularly noteworthy life that, in shining the spotlight on that one life, shows the cultural environment in which the protagonist lived and worked.

Another such programme, *A Life Less Ordinary*, follows the stories of ordinary people caught up in extraordinary events, and gives them a chance to talk about their experience. Among them was Christopher Jefferies, who described the 'emotional earthquake' caused by his treatment in the press following his arrest in connection with the murder of his tenant, Joanna Yeates. Another was Sandra Gregory, who spent seven years in prison in Thailand for attempting to smuggle heroin.

> 66 *There are some really interesting people on* Last Word, *and not always famous or extraordinary in the obvious sense. I often feel after I have listened to the broadcast that I'd liked to have known that person.* 99
>
> **CHRISTINE CLARK, EDITOR**

THE REUNION

PROGRAMME STATS

Running since: 2006

Current presenter: Sue MacGregor

Description: Series which reunites a group of people intimately involved in a moment of modern history.

Website: www.bbc.co.uk/programmes/b007x9vc

Since 2006, Sue MacGregor has been reuniting groups of people who were thrown together for one reason or another – whether by choice (the 1966 World Cup winners) or not (the prisoners incarcerated with Nelson Mandela on Robben Island). She has reunited:

The women involved in the creation of *Spare Rib*, an avant-garde magazine that caught the spirit of the 1970s women's liberation movement. Among them are editors Marsha Rowe and Rosie Boycott, photographer Angela Phillips, and Anna Raeburn, who wrote the advice column.

Five people who recalled their experiences of the German occupation of Jersey.

The key players involved in the Lib-Lab pact of the late 1970s.

Nick Leeson and his boss at Barings Bank.

The cast and producers of several television programmes and films, including:
Goodness Gracious Me
Brideshead Revisited
Four Weddings and a Funeral
Play School
The Navy Lark

In a special hundredth edition recorded in Dallas, Sue MacGregor reunited those who were there when John F. Kennedy was assassinated.

GREAT LIVES

PROGRAMME STATS

Running since: 2001

Current presenter: Matthew Parris (@MatthewParris3)

Past presenters: Joan Bakewell, Humphrey Carpenter, Francine Stock

Description: Biographical series in which guests choose someone who has inspired their lives.

Website: www.bbc.co.uk/programmes/b006qxsb

In each programme a distinguished guest is asked to nominate someone they feel led a great life. Along with an expert on the chosen person (such as a contemporary, biographer or friend), Matthew Parris guides a discussion about their life.

Here is a selection of *Great Lives* nominations from the 2013/2014 series:

Michael Palin	Ernest Hemingway
John Cooper Clarke	Salvador Dalí
Ralph Steadman	Friedrich Nietzsche
Rosie Boycott	Ernest Shackleton
Fay Weldon	H. G. Wells
Evelyn Glennie	Jacqueline du Pré
Sara Cox	Lisa 'Left Eye' Lopes
Julie Burchill	Ava Gardner
Gabriel Gbadamosi	Fela Kuti
Russell Grant	Ivor Novello
Al Murray	Field Marshal Bernard Montgomery

DESERT ISLAND DISCS

PROGRAMME STATS

Running since: 1942

Current host: Kirsty Young (since 2006)

Past hosts: Roy Plomley (1942–1985), Michael Parkinson (1985–1987), Sue Lawley (1988–2006)

Listening figures: 2.99 million (weekly figures from RAJAR for the first quarter of 2014)

The first ever *DID* was broadcast on 29 January 1942, when Roy Plomley's first castaway was actor and comedian (and Winston Churchill's son-in-law) Vic Oliver (1898–1964). As with so many of the guests in the early days, Oliver's selection was almost exclusively classical, and included Chopin, Tchaikovsky and Wagner.

THEIR DISCS

Since 1942 over 22,000 discs have been chosen by castaways. Here are the top choices:

1   Ludvig van Beethoven – Symphony No. 9 in D Minor ('Choral')

2   Sergei Rachmaninov – Piano Concerto No. 2 in C Minor

3   Franz Schubert – String Quintet in C Major

4   Ludvig van Beethoven – Symphony No. 6 in F Major ('Pastoral')

5   Edward Elgar – Pomp and Circumstance March No. 1 in D Major ('Land of Hope and Glory')

6   Ludvig van Beethoven – Piano Concerto No. 5 in E Flat Major ('Emperor')

7   Edward Elgar – Enigma Variations ('Nimrod')

8   Ludvig van Beethoven – Symphony No. 7 in A Major

Note: Because of the way castaways choose their favourites, a symphony counts as one disc, or track, as does one aria from an opera or an oratorio like Handel's *Messiah*.

THEIR LUXURIES

Castaways are permitted to take a luxury item with them onto their island exile, which can be anything at all as long as it has no practical use. Here is a selection of some of the castaways' choices:

Dame Edna Everage	Madge Allsop (1988)
Sheila Hancock	Cat food (1965); a grand piano and music scores (2000)
Alfred Hitchcock	A continental railway timetable (1959)
Neil Kinnock	Radio 4 (1988 – Sue Lawley agreed that he could take a receiver but not a transmitter)
Sue Lawley	An iron and ironing board (1987)
Arthur Scargill	The *Mona Lisa* (1988) (also chosen by Cilla Black in 1964)
Harry Secombe	A collapsible concrete model of Broadcasting House (1956); a guitar (1997)
Barbara Windsor	Hairpieces (1970); writing materials and a Union flag (1990)
Mai Zetterling	A recording of applause (1951)

THE PEOPLE'S ISLAND

In 2011, *DID* listeners were invited to vote for their eight discs. In choosing all but two classical pieces, we turned out to be a surprisingly conservative lot:

1 Ralph Vaughan Williams – 'The Lark Ascending'

2 Sir Edward Elgar – Enigma Variations

3 Ludwig van Beethoven – Symphony No. 9 in D Minor ('Choral')

4 Queen – 'Bohemian Rhapsody'

5 Pink Floyd – 'Comfortably Numb'

6 Sir Edward Elgar – Cello Concerto in E Minor

7 George Frideric Handel – *Messiah*

8 Gustav Holst – The Planets

ROY PLOMLEY (1914–1985)

The programme's creator and presenter for forty-three years, Plomley originally hailed from Wimbledon. When he took part in a locally produced operetta he was left 'stage-struck'.

Despite his theatrical ambitions, acting roles were not forthcoming in Plomley's early career, and he worked for an estate agent, an advertising agency, a publishing company and a man who sold horoscopes by post from an office in Jersey. In 1936, however, an opportunity to work as an announcer and producer for Radio Normandy took him to France, where he and his fiancée Diana married in 1940.

The Plomleys stayed in Paris for a few months, but ended up having to make a dash for it back to England as German occupying forces approached the French capital. It was a narrow escape and they lost all their possessions en route.

Back in England on a cold day in November 1941, Plomley was in his pyjamas and just about to go to bed when a programme idea suddenly came to him. He immediately sat down at his typewriter and sent it to the BBC, and an astonishingly short time later – in January 1942 – he was recording the first programme. And the rest, as they say, is history.

When it came to desert island existence, Plomley confessed that he found the idea of being a castaway terrifying. He said: 'I know... quite a lot about desert islands and I know that they are not places to go to.'

DESERT ISLAND REVELATIONS

James Naughtie has described *DID* as 'the probe that you hardly feel going in'. Sue Lawley has said that the format is 'desperately simple but very clever'.

Here are some examples of castaways' revelations and confessions:

In 1982 Paul McCartney told Roy Plomley that as teenagers he and John Lennon used to sit around smoking Typhoo tea, thinking they were being 'artsy'.

Germaine Greer told Sue Lawley in 1988 that she thought it was 'bliss' not to have to worry about sex any more.

In 2007, Yoko Ono revealed to Kirsty Young that when she had been pregnant with Sean she had been in two minds as to whether to keep the baby.

In an emotional interview with Kirsty Young in 2010, footballer Tony Adams described being reconciled with his parents when he had recovered from alcoholism.

In 2014 Jack Dee revealed that in his early twenties he seriously considered going into the priesthood, until he found out what was wrong with him: 'I'm a comedian.'

CASTAWAY INCIDENTS AND EMBARRASSMENTS

One (unnamed) actor turned up to the studio so drunk that he had to be asked to come back and re-record it the following day sober, which he did.

Actress Lauren Bacall (1979) and film producer Otto Preminger (1980) were both famously abrasive guests for Roy Plomley to deal with.

On one occasion in the early 1970s, an administrative error led to the wrong guest being invited to take part in *DID*. Alistair MacLean the celebrated thriller writer was famously reluctant to be interviewed, so there was elation in the *DID* production office when he agreed to take part in the programme. On the day, however, elation turned to dismay when it wasn't the novelist who turned up at the studio, but Alistair MacLean, the Head of the European office of the Ontario Tourist Bureau. The programme was recorded – apparently he gave a good interview – but it was never broadcast. The 'right' Alistair MacLean never did become a castaway.

Norman Mailer raised eyebrows in 1979 when he requested a stick of the very best marijuana as his desert island luxury. Apparently unfazed, Plomley pointed out: 'This is illegal talk, Mr Mailer.' Surprisingly for the day, the programme was broadcast complete with the drug reference.

In 1996, Sue Lawley asked the then Shadow Chancellor Gordon Brown very directly about his sexuality. She said that people want to know 'whether you're gay or whether there's some flaw in your personality that you haven't made a relationship'. Brown's response was: 'It just hasn't happened.'

In 1989 Sue Lawley interviewed Diana Mosley, widow of wartime fascist leader Oswald Mosley. The interview provoked outrage and hundreds of complaints when Mosley declared that Hitler was 'fascinating' and had 'mesmeric' eyes.

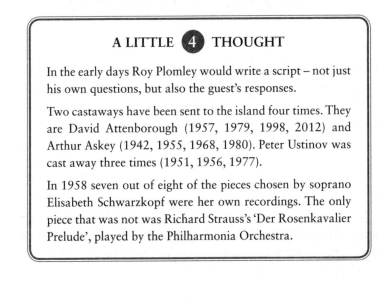

A LITTLE 4 THOUGHT

In the early days Roy Plomley would write a script – not just his own questions, but also the guest's responses.

Two castaways have been sent to the island four times. They are David Attenborough (1957, 1979, 1998, 2012) and Arthur Askey (1942, 1955, 1968, 1980). Peter Ustinov was cast away three times (1951, 1956, 1977).

In 1958 seven out of eight of the pieces chosen by soprano Elisabeth Schwarzkopf were her own recordings. The only piece that was not was Richard Strauss's 'Der Rosenkavalier Prelude', played by the Philharmonia Orchestra.

LISTENER-FOCUSED PROGRAMMING

Broadly, this chapter concerns that part of Radio 4's output which centres – either completely or in part – on the listener. It is a broad church – a mixed and rather lumpy bag of programmes. It encompasses magazine programmes with a phone-in element, such as *Saturday Live*, consumer programmes aimed at a wide audience, such as *You and Yours*, programmes which champion the rights of a specific group, such as *In Touch* and those, like *Feedback*, which give the listener a right to reply.

But whether or not they are interactive, whether their reach is the average UK household or a minority-interest group, these programmes all have in common the fact that the listener is a big part of the programme.

PEOPLE POWER – INTERACTIVITY

SATURDAY LIVE

PROGRAMME STATS

Running since: 2006

Current presenters: Richard Coles with J. P. Devlin (@devlin_jp) and others

Past presenters: Fi Glover, Sian Williams

Description: Extraordinary stories and remarkable people.

Website: www.bbc.co.uk/programmes/b006qgj4

'An avalanche survivor, a mother bent on bilingual children, and the Inheritance Tracks of Judy Finnigan' – there's a sentence you never thought you'd hear. But those were the words with which one episode of *Saturday Live* was announced recently. All that, plus the man who phoned in to tell how he'd lost a bit of an original Banksy artwork, maths writer Alex Bellos, and the man who, at thirteen, met and was photographed with his hero Pelé.

Saturday Live's informal atmosphere takes the listener back to heady, hedonistic student days – a Saturday morning around a kitchen table in shared digs, hangovers temporarily abated in chat that is occasionally raucous, often hilarious, sometimes poignant and always scintillating.

And just in case you thought a maths writer might not make scintillating Saturday morning chat, Alex Bellos talks about Chinese superstitions about the number four, explaining that the word for 'four' sounds like the word for 'death', and it's avoided in much the way the number thirteen is avoided in western culture.

A LITTLE 4 THOUGHT

The story of Saturday Live presenter, the Revd Richard Coles (he is a gay Anglican priest who once topped the charts as a member of the Communards), was an inspiration for the television drama *Rev*, starring Tom Hollander.

THE LISTENING PROJECT

PROGRAMME STATS

Running since: 2014

Current presenter: Fi Glover

Description: Capturing the nation in conversation to build a unique picture of our lives today and preserve it for future generations.

Website: www.bbc.co.uk/listeningproject

An ambitious project served up in bite-sized instalments, the aim of *The Listening Project* initiative, in conjunction with the British Library, is to provide a series of snapshots of contemporary Britain.

In each five-minute episode, two people who are close volunteer to have a conversation about a subject they've never discussed intimately before.

Producers emphasise there is an important distinction here between a conversation and an interview – this is emphatically the former. Conversations are, however, facilitated, and edited from around an hour's conversation to a five-minute programme.

Many of the unedited conversations are being archived by the British Library and used to build up a collection of voices, creating a unique portrait of the UK, including:

Eddie and Leigh – a father and daughter discuss his drug addiction.

Charlotte and Peta – two friends reunited by a tragic loss.

Iris and Sid – newlyweds in their nineties, who met at a bus stop.

Conversations can be downloaded and uploaded at www.bbc.co.uk/listeningproject.

HOME TRUTHS

An honourable mention goes to *Home Truths* with John Peel – a true man of the people. Essentially a talk show where Peel 'met' ordinary people with extraordinary stories, it was launched as part of James Boyle's 1998 schedule changes.

At that time Peel was still a rather subversive figure, associated in many people's minds with unlistenable music made by unsavoury musicians. At the same time, however, he had been a Radio 4 presence since 1996, from when he had fronted *Offspring*, which helped him make the transition to homespun radio personality. *Offspring* had a similar format to *Home Truths*, but its focus was mainly children. For example, Peel spoke to a nine-year-old boy who acted as a carer for his severely epileptic mother.

The programme had that Saturday morning freewheeling feel – the kind of programme you could dip in and out of as you sat around the kitchen table over a late and leisurely breakfast, occasionally raising an eyebrow over the top of the weekend papers.

Where the Radio 4 listener's great talent is curiosity, for Peel it was a superpower. He could be surprised, and even bemused by some of the stories he heard, but he never stooped to ridicule or sarcasm. There was the woman who associated words with food, for example: 'Thelma's a vegetable marrow... I've got a lot of Yorkshire pudding names – Jennifer's a Yorkshire pudding name.' Together they established that John Peel added up to 'custard, Aspro tablets and chips'.

After Peel's death in 2004, *Home Truths* survived until 2006, with Linda Smith and Tom Robinson among others stepping into the breach. But Peel proved to be an impossible act to follow and the format was eventually replaced by *Saturday Live*.

PESTER POWER – FEEDBACK PROGRAMMING

FEEDBACK

PROGRAMME STATS

Running since: 1979

Current presenter: Roger Bolton

Past presenters: Chris Dunkley, Susan Marling, Colin Semper, Mary Whitehouse

Description: Radio 4's forum for comments, queries, criticisms and congratulations.

Website: www.bbc.co.uk/programmes/b006slnx

Twitter: @BBCR4Feedback

Feedback ponderings include:

Was it insensitive to broadcast Ruth Archer's miscarriage on Mother's Day?

Is 6.30 p.m. the time for jokes about group sex in parks?

Is there too much Nigella on Radio 4?

Is Radio 4 trying to scare listeners senseless?

A LITTLE 4 THOUGHT

Astonishingly, Mary Whitehouse was a temporary presenter of *Feedback* in the mid 1980s.

The forerunner to *Feedback* was called *Disgusted, Tunbridge Wells*, introduced in 1978.

PURCHASE POWER – CONSUMER PROGRAMMING

YOU AND YOURS

PROGRAMME STATS

Running since: 1970

Current presenters: Peter White or Winifred Robinson

Past presenters: Liz Barclay, Sue Cook, Derek Cooper, Paul Heiney, John Waite, Nancy Wise, Julian Worricker, Joan Yorke

Description: News and discussion of consumer affairs.

Related programme: *Face the Facts*

Website: www.bbc.co.uk/programmes/b006qps9

The 1970s was the decade of consumer empowerment, with programmes such as *You and Yours* either following or leading the trend depending on your point of view (in truth, it was probably a bit of both).

After nearly half a century, *You and Yours* has got into its groove. Hackers, scammers, fraudsters, rip-off merchants and faceless corporations are all taken to task by Winifred Robinson and Peter White, acting on behalf of the hacked, the scammed, the defrauded and the ripped-off.

Although it has been comfortably ensconced in its lunchtime slot since the beginning, *Y&Y* has known format changes over the years. In the great reorganisation of 1998, for example, it more than doubled in length, from 25 to 55 minutes. Then in 2008 it underwent a change in its format, when two presenters (per programme) were replaced by one. In addition, its range of topics has been widened to include medical as well as consumer issues – for example, caring for people with cancer, dementia or diabetes.

A LITTLE ④ THOUGHT

Occasionally an item on *Y&Y* really stretches the definition of what counts as consumer programming – such as Billy Bragg discussing whether England should have a new National Anthem. (Vox pop suggestions included songs by Kate Bush and Ivor Novello, and the Sex Pistols' 'God Save the Queen'.)

MONEY BOX

PROGRAMME STATS

Running since: 1977

Current presenter: Paul Lewis (@paullewismoney)

Past presenters: Louise Botting (1977–1992), Naga Munchetty

Listening figures: 1.2 million (weekly figures from RAJAR for the first quarter of 2014)

Description: The latest news from the world of personal finance plus advice for those trying to make the most of their money.

Related programme: *Money Box Live* with Vincent Duggleby or Paul Lewis

Website: www.bbc.co.uk/programmes/b006qjnv

Mortgages, taxes, savings, pensions, care fees, benefits and banks – all financial life is here. In *Money Box* Paul Lewis invites guests to explain the intricacies of the financial world, while its sister programme *Money Box Live* gives listeners a chance to put their specific questions to a panel of experts.

A LITTLE **4** THOUGHT

Besides being a financial journalist, Paul Lewis is an authority on the Victorian novelist Wilkie Collins, whom he describes as a 'superstar of Victorian fiction'.

PHYSICAL POWER – DISABILITY PROGRAMMING

Of course not all disability programming on Radio 4 is listener-centred. There are many excellent documentaries, for example, which bring us stories about and insights into disability, such as *Disability: A New History* and *No Triumph, No Tragedy*.

But on Radio 4 in particular, consumer and disability programming are brought together in the person of Peter White – presenter of *You and Yours* as well as being the BBC's Disability Affairs Correspondent.

IN TOUCH

PROGRAMME STATS

Running since: 1961

Current presenter: Peter White (since 1974)

Description: Peter White with news and information for blind and partially sighted people.

Website: www.bbc.co.uk/programmes/b006qxww

A ukulele band at a school for the visually impaired in Liverpool, changes to disabled students' allowances, cycling for the blind, an interview with author Sue Townsend, Peter White goes to the races – just a few of the items covered over a few programmes of *In Touch*.

A mixture of interviews, investigation and news is packed into this twenty-minute programme, which has a loyal following among blind and visually impaired people, but also appeals to many sighted people because it's, well, just interesting.

In 2011, 'Can't See Will Cook' was a short series of cookery programmes forming part of *In Touch*. Blind foodie Peter Lane either cooked a gourmet dish himself, or met another keen amateur chef to find out about their favourite dish and how they get round the drawbacks of being visually impaired in the kitchen. Recipes included cakes, curries, pies, Lebanese dishes and a Christmas nut roast.

The '*In Touch* In-Tray' is an occasional series within *In Touch*, which answers questions such as 'How do you keep reading when you're losing your sight?' and 'What are the most usable dating websites when you're blind?'

WOMEN ON RADIO 4

THE ROLE OF WOMEN ON RADIO 4

Radio is, of course, a product of its age, and, as might be expected, the role of women in the early days was largely confined to the realm of the domestic. They might comment on 'household matters', for example, or talk about their garden or travels, or appear as one of the 'aunts' on *Children's Hour*.

Sometimes they would be women with high public profiles – Vita Sackville-West and Rebecca West had plenty of airtime. But for all that women might have been taken seriously as writers at the time, as announcers or newsreaders their voices were not deemed to have the necessary authority for the job.

So it comes as a bit of a surprise to learn that the first voice of a female announcer – that of Sheila Borrett – was heard on the Home Service as early as 1933. Of course it did not go unremarked, with the *Radio Times* predicting 'panic among the horsehair armchairs, retired colonels muttering darkly over their muffins'. In the event it was not the colonels, but mostly women listeners who wrote in to complain, and the experiment was abandoned after three months.

On the other hand, there have been women working behind the microphone since the earliest days of the Home Service and

Radio 4. Some of them, such as Monica Sims, rose right to the top. Sims was editor of *Woman's Hour* between 1964 and 1968, and went on to become Controller of Radio 4 from 1978 until 1983.

Yet it was not until 1972 that the first female newsreader's voice, that of Hylda Bamber, was heard on Radio 4. And even then, it would seem, there was still a lot of nervousness about such a radical move – she was axed after six months.

However, the women's lib movement was in full swing and the notion that a woman's voice did not have sufficient authority was dead in the water. In 1974 Radio 4 appointed the first permanent female newsreader – Sheila Tracy.

Nowadays it is a truth almost universally acknowledged that women can more than hold their own in the fast-paced world of radio broadcasting, and can stand up to the most difficult of interviewees.

Even so, in 2010 the editor of *Today*, Ceri Thomas, came under fire for appearing to suggest that the programme was too tough an environment for women to work in. And when in 2014 Mishal Husain became the fourth female presenter on *Today*, the tabloids went into overdrive about the sex appeal in her voice, with the *Daily Mail* describing it as 'deliciously delicate and feminine... little wonder men up and down the country are reaching for their radio "on" buttons'. Husain manages to hold her own, however, despite this kind of sexism – as do countless women at Radio 4.

A LITTLE 4 THOUGHT

In swing-music circles, Sheila Tracy's fame as the first female newsreader on Radio 4 is surpassed by her fame as a musician – she is a first-rate and much acclaimed trombonist.

There have been four female controllers of Radio 4 to date: Clare Lawson Dick (1975–1976), Monica Sims (1978–1983), Helen Boaden (2000–2004) and Gwyneth Williams (2010–present).

On 10 October 2013, the *Today* programme was fronted by four women for the first time. With Mishal Husain and Sarah Montague presenting, Corrie Corfield read the news and Alison Mitchell the sport. It was not however an all-female line-up, as Simon Jack was presenting the business news.

WOMAN'S HOUR

PROGRAMME STATS

Running since: 1946

Current hosts: Jenni Murray (@whjm) and Jane Garvey (@janegarvey1)

Past hosts include: Marjorie Anderson, Violet Carson, Judith Chalmers, Joan Griffiths, Alan Ivimey, Martha Kearney (1998–2007), Sue MacGregor (1972–1987), Jean Metcalfe, Olive Shapley

Listening figures: 3.68 million (weekly figures from RAJAR for the first quarter of 2014)

Related programme: *Weekend Woman's Hour* (4–5 p.m. Saturday)

Description: The programme that offers a female perspective on the world.

Website: www.bbc.co.uk/programmes/b007qlvb

Twitter: @BBCWomansHour

Of all the programmes to have undergone the greatest transformation during the lifetime of Radio 4, *Woman's Hour* is surely up there in the top three.

Created by Controller of the Light Programme Norman Collins, *Woman's Hour* was first broadcast in 1946. It was scheduled at 2 p.m., after a woman's housework was finished, but before the children came home from school. Early episodes featured items such as 'Cooking with whale meat', 'I married a lion tamer' and 'How to hang your husband's suit'.

But although it was the product of a man's world – created and (initially) presented by men who thought they knew what women wanted and needed – *Woman's Hour* was never, as has been suggested, a completely lightweight programme intended to occupy the housewife while she did her chores. Interviewed in 1967 (and, it has to be said, possibly on the defensive)

Collins reminisced that his original idea had been to introduce a programme that emphasised 'the intelligence of the woman, because I really do think... the intelligence of the woman is underrated'.

From the outset, Collins claimed, he intended *Woman's Hour* to be a vehicle for serious topics of interest to both genders, interspersed with a little light music. As he revealed in 1967, 'Secretly I always hoped that there would be more talk and less light music.'

Possibly this was partly why, according to the BBC History website, from the outset BBC managers were panicking about the idea of the menopause being discussed on *Woman's Hour*. Their nightmare – and worse – came true during the 1960s when cookery, gardening and needlework gave way to a range of topics that even now sound alarming. In *The Radio Companion*, Paul Donovan lists some of them as: 'Masturbation, homosexuality, the Pill, frigidity, transsexuality, impotence and flatulence – complete with sound effects.'

A LITTLE 4 THOUGHT

Woman's Hour's first presenter was a man – journalist and ex-RAF intelligence officer Alan Ivimey, who 'specialised in writing for and talking to women'.

On 1 January 2005, the *Woman's Hour* show became *Man's Hour* for one episode only, when it was presented by Jon Snow.

The first-ever episode of *Woman's Hour* featured Labour politician and feminist Margaret Bondfield, Hollywood actress Deborah Kerr and Mrs Elsie Crump, a butcher's wife.

WOMEN ON THE MARCH

In 1973 *Woman's Hour* transferred from Radio 2 to Radio 4, where it occupied an afternoon slot until 1991. During its long run, its presenters have interviewed thousands of women from all walks of life: from Enid Blyton to Doris Lessing, Nancy Astor to Doreen Lawrence, Lillian Gish to Jane Fonda, Billie Jean King to Tanni Grey-Thompson.

Many of them are high-profile figures in entertainment, politics, the arts and more, while others, such as Kate McCann whose daughter Madeleine was abducted in 2007, or Michelle Knight who was kept captive for eleven years by Ariel Castro, have found themselves in the limelight in ways they never sought.

FROM THE *WOMAN'S HOUR* COLLECTION:

Suffragette Mary Richardson recalling in 1957 how she watched Emily Davison edging herself towards the rails on the day she threw herself in front of the King's horse at the 1913 Epsom Derby: 'There she stood, tall, erect, calm, though she knew that within a short half-hour she would surrender her life.'

Judi Dench's revelation in 1967 that she wanted to be a stage designer but went into acting when she realised she wasn't going to be very good at it.

A 1971 interview with Mary Quant who – to the obvious amusement of the presenter – turned up in the studio wearing ex-Army gear.

Sue MacGregor's 1986 interview with Winnie Mandela in her Soweto home, against an audio backdrop of barking police dogs.

Jenni Murray's 1993 interview with Margaret Thatcher, in which the former prime minister revealed that she felt 'sick at heart' after being deserted by her Cabinet. Murray later said she had been 'terrified' and noted that one reviewer said that 'his radio had frozen over'.

The 1999 episode in which Julie Burchill and Germaine Greer clashed while they were discussing female genital mutilation. Martha Kearney later recalled that they threw away the rest of the running order and let the two women fight it out.

A LITTLE **4** THOUGHT

According to figures published in the last quarter of 2013, 60.8 per cent of *Woman's Hour* listeners were female and 39.2 per cent were male.

WOMAN'S HOUR TAKEOVER

In April and May 2014, J. K. Rowling was the first of a series of five guest editors of *Woman's Hour*, followed by Kelly Holmes, Naomi Alderman, Doreen Lawrence and Lauren Laverne.

JENNI MURRAY

Jenni Murray was born in Barnsley in 1950. One of her earliest memories of *Woman's Hour* is listening with her mother on the family's Bush radio, and being sent to the kitchen on 'errands' whenever an item carrying a 'health warning' came on.

She joined BBC Radio Bristol in 1973 and went on to report and present for *South Today* on BBC TV. In 1983 she joined *Newsnight*, where she spent two years before moving to the *Today* programme on Radio 4. From there she took up the *Woman's Hour* baton from Sue MacGregor in 1987.

At the end of a programme in 2006, Murray announced that she had been diagnosed with breast cancer. She said that her prognosis was good, and did indeed return to the programme a few months later, although the aggressive chemotherapy treatment she underwent meant that she needed two hip replacements in 2008.

In 2010 she won a Sony Award for her interview with Sharon Shoesmith, the Head of Children's Services at Haringey Council who had been dismissed in 2008 over the death of 'Baby P'.

THINGS YOU (PROBABLY) NEVER KNEW ABOUT *WOMAN'S HOUR* PRESENTERS PAST AND PRESENT

Jane Garvey started her broadcasting career in local radio in 1987, living in a bedsit and earning £2,600 a year.

Violet Carson (1898–1983), who presented *Woman's Hour* for five years in the 1950s, is probably better known to *Coronation Street* fans as Ena Sharples.

After a flirtation with Communism as a young woman, Olive Shapley (1910–1999) continued to get regular visits from MI5 into her sixties. She said she looked forward to the officer's visit and 'always made him a pot of tea'.

> **66** *Woman's Hour is like a stately galleon in full sail... far bigger than anyone who will ever present it.* **99**
>
> **JANE GARVEY**

66 *In the 1980s we had a weird mixture of knit-a-royal-corgi and radical Guardian Women's Page feminism. It was like that in the real world, and it was reflected on Woman's Hour!* 99

VIV BOARDMAN, BACKGROUND ACTOR AND MUSIC AGENT

66 *I have always loathed Woman's Hour, which seems obsessed with feminism and gynaecology.* 99

PRUDENCE DAILEY, CHAIRMAN, PRAYER BOOK SOCIETY

SCIENCE AND NATURE

An odd assortment of programmes jostle together in this chapter – not least, of course, because everything has a scientific angle. So medical science and psychiatry go under the same umbrella as mathematics, farming, gardening and astronomy.

HOME ON THE FARM

Although farming matters were discussed from time to time on BBC Radio in the very early days, it was not until 1929 that a farming programme was introduced into the daily schedule, in the form of the Fatstock Prices. According to Paul Donovan, the solemn recitation 'became something of a music hall joke'.

When producer John Green joined the BBC from the Ministry of Agriculture, it created a link which still exists between the BBC and Whitehall. In the 1930s he introduced the programme *For Farmers Only*, only for it to be axed at the outbreak of war in 1939. Once the value of farming for the war effort had been recognised, however, there was a scramble to introduce programmes that would help farmers boost productivity and keep the nation fed. Indeed, it was soon considered so important that the government wanted direct control over farming broadcasting. In the end, an advisory body was established, further strengthening the link between Whitehall and the BBC.

Today, Radio 4's output chiefly comprises the two early-morning strands *Farming Today*, broadcast every day from Monday to Saturday, with *On Your Farm* on a Sunday morning. The latter is billed as 'Getting to the heart of country life with a look at individual farming endeavours', and essentially involves a visit to a different farm each week, to meet farmers and look at different farming methods.

A LITTLE **4** THOUGHT

One of the key figures in the early days of BBC Radio's farming programming was Anthony Hurd, father of the politician Douglas Hurd.

When BBC Television broadcast the first news bulletin in 1954, its critics said it was 'as visually impressive as the Fatstock Prices'.

FARMING TODAY

PROGRAMME STATS

Running since: 1937, in one form or another

Current presenters/producers: Sarah Falkingham, Caz Graham, Anna Hill, Charlotte Smith, Sarah Swadling

Past presenters: Miriam O'Reilly, Mark Holdstock

Description: The latest news about food, farming and the countryside.

Website: www.bbc.co.uk/programmes/b006qj8q

Farming Today explores issues of current concern to farmers, fishermen and anyone with an interest in countryside issues. An episode can be jam-packed with a diverse range of topics. Some recent examples include:

'Space salad', factory farming and encouraging children as budding farmers.

Offal exports, rare bees and newcomers to farming.

Art in the fields, mussel-farming ban and dairy genetics.

Dog faeces, pig farrowing crates and farmed fish.

A LITTLE  THOUGHT

Producer Sarah Falkingham puts the popularity of *Farming Today* at least in part down to the foot-and-mouth outbreak of 2001. She says: 'There's no doubting that the crisis built the audience.'

It's said that at least two prime ministers – Margaret Thatcher and Gordon Brown – regularly tuned in to *Farming Today* when they were in office.

In 2014 *Farming Today*'s April Fool prank was the announcement that giraffe's milk was going on sale.

THE NATURAL WORLD

Since the foundation of the Natural History Unit in Bristol in 1957, the BBC has forged a place for itself as the world's leading producer and broadcaster of natural history.

For a while after 1979, when David Attenborough's astonishing *Life on Earth* burst onto our screens and showed nature in all its vibrant glory, it must have seemed that television had the edge over radio. But radio, characteristically unassuming, found a way to stand its ground, and some truly remarkable nature programming has reached us over the airwaves. Challenged by the restrictions of radio, producers learnt how to use the voices of people – presenters, experts or enthusiasts – and the sounds of nature – a lamb being born, a bird call, an ice shelf cracking – to bring an aural landscape to life for the listener.

What's more, radio isn't just about working with the challenges of technological limitations. Microphones can often be deployed where cameras cannot – such as deep in the trenches of the Pacific Ocean.

And when it comes to bringing nature to our ears there is, arguably, no finer example than something a little bird – literally – told us...

TWEET OF THE DAY

For a year, *Tweet of the Day* listeners felt like the proverbial early birds who'd caught the worm. Made by the radio division of the BBC's Natural History Unit in Bristol, it was broadcast from May 2013, and aired between 5.58 and 6 a.m. on weekdays. *Tweet* presenters included Michaela Strachan, Chris Packham, Kate Humble and David Attenborough.

Usually, each tiny-yet-perfectly-formed programme focused on a type of bird – not only its call, but its habits, ornithology and place in folklore.

For example, David Attenborough presents the story of the whimbrel, a close relation of the curlew. In just 90 seconds he explains that it breeds in the far north and overwinters in southern Europe and Africa. On its way north again in late April and May, the whimbrel's migration path takes it over the Midlands. Although only a fleeting visitor flying overhead at night, its distinctive seven-note call gave rise to a legend about the 'six birds of fate' that were constantly seeking the seventh. When all seven were united, the legend had it, the world would end.

In 2014, to mark International Dawn Chorus Day, a series of dawn choruses were recorded from different locations (urban, wetland, woodland). This formed part of a project to allow the children of the Royal London Children's Hospital to hear the wildlife sounds on their doorstep. Birds featured included the robin, blackbird, great tit and house sparrow.

Like all the best series, *Tweet* developed a loyal following. As executive producer Julian Hector explained: 'Finally, what came through... was the huge effect birds have on us and our daily lives.'

RAMBLINGS

PROGRAMME STATS

Current presenter: Clare Balding

Description: Programme in which the presenter joins notable and interesting people on a walk through the countryside.

Website: www.bbc.co.uk/programmes/b006xrr2

Clare has rambled through many different landscapes, from the remote and rural to urban parkland – the Wicklow Mountains, Cardiff, the Lake District, Hampshire and Richmond Park in London.

Along the way she's been accompanied by a wide range of walkers – from a group of taxidermists in Boston Spa, to former punk queen Toyah Willcox in Worcestershire. She's rambled around the green spaces of Sheffield, talking to refugees and asylum seekers as they improve their English and discover more about their new home.

SCIENCE

Among Radio 4's dedicated science strands are:

Frontiers Exploring new ideas in science and meeting the scientists and researchers responsible for them, as well as hearing from their critics.

Inside Science Adam Rutherford and guests illuminate the mysteries and challenge the controversies behind the science that's changing our world.

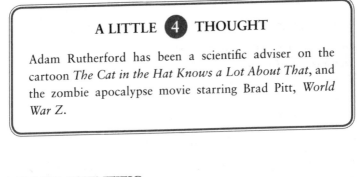

A LITTLE 4 THOUGHT

Adam Rutherford has been a scientific adviser on the cartoon *The Cat in the Hat Knows a Lot About That*, and the zombie apocalypse movie starring Brad Pitt, *World War Z*.

THE LIFE SCIENTIFIC

PROGRAMME STATS

Current presenter: Jim Al-Khalili

Description: Talking to leading scientists about their life and work, finding out what inspires and motivates them, and asking what their discoveries might do for mankind.

Website: www.bbc.co.uk/programmes/b015sqc7

Jim Al-Khalili is evangelical about the work he does, and wants to introduce audiences to – in his own words – 'mind-blowing big ideas and concepts'.

A theoretical nuclear physicist by training, Al-Khalili has presented *The Life Scientific* since 2011. In each programme he talks to a prominent figure from the world of science, in its broadest sense. He might meet a natural scientist, a mathematician, an engineer or an expert in technology, medicine or the social sciences. His guests have included Nobel Prize winners, government advisers, writers and other people who have made a contribution to our understanding of the universe.

Some examples from the 2014 series are:

Child psychiatrist Michael Rutter

Chief Scientist for the Met Office Julia Slingo

Entomologist Janet Hemingway on the war on malaria

Veronica van Heyningen, a world leader in the genetics of the development of the eye

---

A LITTLE 4 THOUGHT

Al-Khalili has likened *The Life Scientific* to '*Desert Island Discs* without the discs'.

THE INFINITE MONKEY CAGE

PROGRAMME STATS

Running since: 2009

Current presenters: Robin Ince (@robinince), Brian Cox (@ProfBrianCox)

Description: Witty, irreverent look at the world through scientists' eyes.

Website: www.bbc.co.uk/programmes/b00snr0w

Twitter: @themonkeycage

Science at its most accessible and entertaining, each show takes a topic – the apocalypse, space travel – and invites a panel of scientists and a motley crew of guests (such as Katy Brand, Graeme Garden, Dave Gorman, Claudia Hammond, Eric Idle, Josie Long and Ross Noble) to thrash it out.

A LITTLE (4) THOUGHT

A committed atheist, for Christmas 2008 Robin Ince organised 'Nine Lessons and Carols for Godless People'.

MORE OR LESS

PROGRAMME STATS

Running since: 2001

Current presenter: Tim Harford (@TimHarford)

Past presenter: Andrew Dilnot

Description: Tim Harford explains – and sometimes debunks – the numbers and statistics used in political debate, the news and everyday life.

Website: www.bbc.co.uk/programmes/b006qshd

Started as a one-off series of six programmes, *More or Less* was an instant hit and is still going. It is a wonderful antidote to the sensationalist claims we read in the tabloid headlines. It delves into the figures themselves and their origins, and often finds them to be sloppy, spurious, obsolete or just plain wrong.

In the wake of controversial comments made by UKIP leader Nigel Farage in the run-up to the 2014 European elections, for example, *More or Less* looked at statistics connected with crime committed by Romanian immigrants in the UK. It established that, of three statistical claims quoted by UKIP in *The Telegraph*, one was nearly true (although two years out of date), one was 'a bit weird', and the third was just wrong.

The programme has also looked at claims connected with 'food bank Britain', the EU, the 'ticking time bomb' of obesity, and the controversial Channel 4 documentary *Benefits Street*.

A LITTLE 4 THOUGHT

In 2010 *More or Less* won the Royal Statistical Society's award for Statistical Excellence in Journalism, as well as an award from Mensa, for 'promoting intelligence in public life'.

MEDICAL SCIENCE

Medical matters on Radio 4 are often covered within a magazine programme (such as *Woman's Hour*) or seen in a political or economic context (such as *File on 4* examining the NHS).

Some programmes look at medicine from a historical perspective. In 2010, for example, *A Brave New Life* marked the 200th anniversary of homeopathy's founding text *Samuel Hahnemann's Organon of Rational Medicine*). Other programmes take an investigative angle. Between 2007 and 2011, Vivienne Parry presented eight series of *Am I Normal?*, looking at how doctors decide what is normal and what is not.

ALL IN THE MIND

PROGRAMME STATS

Current presenter: Claudia Hammond (@claudiahammond)

Past presenters: Tanya Byron, Anthony Clare, Kwame McKenzie, Raj Persaud

Description: Programme exploring the limits and potential of the human mind.

Website: www.bbc.co.uk/programmes/b006qxx9

All in the Mind has covered topics such as:

The impact of future health reforms on mental health services.

The psychology of online dating.

HMP Grendon, the only prison in Europe that runs as a therapeutic community.

Assessment of the possibility of a vaccine against depression.

Depressive illness, ecotherapy, and the evidence for 'green therapy'.

GARDENERS' QUESTION TIME

PROGRAMME STATS

Running since: 1947

Current hosts: Eric Robson (@stridingedge) with Peter Gibbs

Regular panellists: Chris Beardshaw (@chrisbeardshaw), Matthew Biggs (@plantmadman), Bob Flowerdew, Pippa Greenwood (@PippaGreenwood), Bunny Guinness, Roy Lancaster, Anne Swithinbank, Christine Walkden (@ChristineWalkd), Matthew Wilson (@LandscapeMan)

Past hosts include: Michael Barratt, Stefan Buczacki, Franklin Engelmann, Ken Ford, Clay Jones, Bob Stead

Listening figures: 1.53 million (weekly figures from RAJAR for the first quarter of 2014)

Website: www.bbc.co.uk/programmes/b006qp2f

Twitter: @BBCGQT

PUTTING DOWN ROOTS

Although the seeds were originally sown in a shaded corner of BBC Radio, *Gardeners' Question Time* proved to be a hardy variety that put down roots, and has flourished and spread over nearly seventy years.

From the outset, there had been gardening programmes on BBC Radio in the form of talks by the likes of Vita Sackville-West, but they lacked the popular touch. The wartime Dig for Victory campaign had bred a generation of keen amateur gardeners and *GQT* – or *How Does Your Garden Grow?*, as it was then called – was a response to the growing trend.

The brainchild of producer Robert Stead, it was originally broadcast in the BBC North region. The first episode aired on

9 April 1947, when the panel took questions from members of the Smallshaw Allotments Association from Ashton-under-Lyne. Stead chaired the programme, and the four-strong panel included commercial grower Bill Sowerbutts and head gardener Fred Loads, who would themselves become hardy perennials on the panel.

In 1951 Professor Alan Gemmell of Keele University joined Sowerbutts and Loads. At the same time the programme moved to Sunday at 2 p.m. and was retitled *Gardeners' Question Time*. Despite its budding popularity, however, it would be six years before it went national. When it did, it quickly became a Sunday lunchtime fixture – partly due to the abrasive banter between the three panellists, with their thick brogues (Sowerbutts and Loads were Lancastrian and Gemmell was a Scot) and different approaches to gardening.

GQT's thousandth programme was broadcast in 1972, by which time it and the panellists were a national institution. Over time, however, the old team broke up, with Bill Sowerbutts making his last appearance in 1983. Thereafter, the panel had an entirely different look, with the likes of Stefan Buczacki, Geoffrey Smith and first female panellist Daphne Ledward.

TROUBLE IN THE GARDEN

In 1994, the normally mild-mannered *GQT* became embroiled in the 'Producer Choice' row that was affecting the entire BBC, and indeed the whole of broadcasting, in the aftermath of the 1990 Broadcasting Act.

As part of the 'deregulation' moves, *GQT* became one of the first programmes to be outsourced to an independent producer (Taylor Made Broadcast). This coincided with Clay Jones's retirement due to ill health, and there was a great deal of speculation in the papers – particularly the *Daily Mail* – as to who the new chairman would be (some of the more outlandish suggestions included Prince Charles and the Bishop of Durham). Controller of Radio 4 Michael Green knew Eric Robson from their days together on *File on 4*, and signed him up. A short while into Robson's chairmanship, however, he received a call from Green to say that he didn't have a panel to work with. Evidently, bad feeling at the move to Taylor Made had boiled over into disagreements between panellists and producers, and the entire panel had defected to Classic FM to start a new gardening show.

According to Robson, Green was so incensed that he 'ditched the shows that were already in the can, and booked the biggest village hall he could lay his hands on' – a concert studio in Manchester. He then invited the *Daily Mail* to witness the success of the new-look programme. The panel included Bob Flowerdew, Pippa Greenwood and Anne Swithinbank – and the *Mail* gave it a thumbs up.

In 2009 the production of the show was taken over by independent production company Somethin' Else. Although the producers have had their detractors, this time the panel has not defected. Nearly seventy years on, and with well over thirty gardening questions answered each week, the show still occupies the Sunday 2 p.m. slot and attracts a weekly listening audience of one and a half million.

As Eric Robson observes:

The listening demographic has changed dramatically in the twenty years I've been presenting the programme. People used to take to gardening when they retired, but now I notice many more women, particularly young women, in the audience. In certain parts of the country we may draw Asian mothers, for example, who are growing things they can't source elsewhere – and they, like everyone else, are concerned to feed their children on good-quality produce.

A LITTLE **4** THOUGHT

In 2010, Bob Flowerdew, Anne Swithinbank and Roy Lancaster broadcast *GQT* from the Central Council of British Naturism in south London. They posed naked (with leaves strategically placed) for publicity shots before responding to questions on a variety of gardening topics from the group of 250 assembled naturists, 240 of whom were naked.

Unusual *GQT* locations have included Leyhill Open Prison, the Palace of Westminster, a London Underground station, the Met Office in Exeter, the Nissan car factory in Sunderland, and on board the Settle to Carlisle Railway.

For the first forty-seven years of the show, *GQT* panel members were shown the questions in advance, but that was dropped in 1994, and the first time a panellist hears the question is when it's asked from the floor.

GQT CONTROVERSIES

In February 2008 a politically incorrect term for *Rhodochiton volubilis*, and the panel's subsequent giggly innuendo-filled discussion, led to accusations of 'offensive racial stereotyping'.

In June 2010 animal rights activists objected to the programme dispensing advice on killing moles, squirrels and rats – the programme's position was vigorously defended by Bunny Guinness and Bob Flowerdew.

In September 2011 former host Professor Stefan Buczacki made a swingeing attack on the programme in the *Daily Mail*, calling it 'a pathetic shadow of its former self' and claiming it had become 'showbiz'.

Portrait of the Presenter As a Listener
ERIC ROBSON
Host, *Gardeners' Question Time*

I did listen to GQT before I worked on it... although I'm no great gardener myself. But that's the point of being the chairman – my job is to keep the experts out of the darker recesses of horticultural Latin.

When I'm not working I listen to... anything and everything. I do a lot of driving and my car radio is welded to Radio 4. I listen to *File on 4*, partly because of my association with it, but also because most weeks it's an excellent bit of reportage. I also like *Feedback*, because it's good to know what your audience is thinking on a broader range of topics. *The Media Show* is very good, and *Test Match Special* is a firm favourite.

THINGS YOU (PROBABLY) NEVER KNEW ABOUT *GQT* PERSONALITIES

Bob Flowerdew lists 'chicken giblet washer', 'dog impersonator' and 'cook in house of ill repute' among his previous occupations.

Peter Gibbs spent two years working and living at the British Halley base on the Brunt Ice Shelf in Antarctica, from where he made weather observations and balloon soundings and helped with routine maintenance in temperatures as low as minus 40 °C.

Pippa Greenwood was the gardening consultant for the ITV murder mystery series *Rosemary and Thyme*, starring Pam Ferris and Felicity Kendal. Her job was to advise on the gardening subplot and other plant-related matters.

Bunny Guinness originally planned a career in science and embarked upon a degree in applied science at Reading University. She swapped courses because she hated spending so much time in the laboratory.

Eric Robson commentated on numerous state occasions in the 1980s for both television and radio – among them US President Jimmy Carter's visit to the north-east of England, the Trooping of the Colour, the Remembrance Day service from the Cenotaph, and Princess Diana's funeral.

Christine Walkden was so worried about how the television series about her, *Christine's Garden*, would be received, that she made sure she was abroad when it was first screened. When she arrived back she was genuinely surprised to find herself 'machine-gunned' with compliments and positive feedback.

RELIGION AND ETHICS

AUNTIE BEEB KNOWS BEST

Back in the day, Auntie Beeb was characterised as a maiden aunt; austere, prudish and remote, she meant well but wasn't really on your wavelength, her wisdom was most definitely dispensed from above, and one of her chief aunt duties was to direct her listeners in religion and ethics.

Nobody is more firmly associated with Auntie Beeb than John Reith. Reith firmly believed that the company (as it was styled until 1927) should be the nation's 'guide, philosopher and friend', and up until he left the corporation (as it had become) in 1938, he did his bit to shape it as such.

As the nation's guide, the BBC under Reith imparted high-minded Christian values. Its first duty was to be edifying and instructional and to lead people to right-thinking and right-doing. Indeed, many would argue that is still the case.

The Reithian philosophy was reinforced during World War Two, when the need for consensus was greater than ever. Post-war, however (much to Reith's dismay), the BBC has had to adapt to modernity and the challenges that come with broadcasting in an age of secularisation, multiculturalism and the permissive society.

Auntie Beeb is indisputably a much more modern aunt these days – less a guide and more a friend. But while she may be far less censorious and controlling than she once was, she still knows what's best for you – and that is a good, solid all-round education, which will equip you to make your own responsible choices in life.

A LITTLE **4** THOUGHT

In the days of the Home Service, no transmission was permitted before 12.30 p.m. on a Sunday, so people were not discouraged from going to church. Even then, Sunday afternoon programming was restricted to religion and classical music.

JOHN REITH (1889–1971)

Reith was born in Glasgow, where his father was a minister. Given how strongly he is associated with the BBC, it comes as something of a surprise to learn that he was there for only sixteen years. During that time, however, his austere Presbyterian upbringing and ethos pervaded the organisation, and arguably helped to shape British culture even today.

He saw his work at the helm of the BBC as a moral mission 'to lead, and to withstand modern laxities, vulgarities, immorality and irreligion and all'. He had a puritanical zeal for unflinchingly telling 'the truth... nothing but the truth', and documented it in his diaries with the kind of journalistic integrity that the BBC has always aspired to.

A LITTLE **4** THOUGHT

Nobody knows for sure how the moniker 'Auntie Beeb' came about, although one story credits both Peter Sellers and Kenny Everett. Peter Sellers is said to have nicknamed it 'Beeb Beeb Ceeb' and when Kenny Everett came along he started referring to 'Auntie Beeb'.

THE RELIGIOUS SCHEDULE ON RADIO 4

A glance at the Radio 4 Religion and Ethics web pages shows traditional Christian broadcasting listed alongside a variety of programmes concerned with ethical issues – some of them fairly heavyweight. It's a mix which does not by any means sit easily with everyone, with many Radio 4 listeners objecting to the implied endorsement of the establishment and established religion. On the other hand, some conservative listeners think that Radio 4 has gone too far towards inclusivity, and should celebrate and endorse Britain as a Christian country.

But despite protests from atheists, humanists, republicans and others, Radio 4 doggedly pursues a broadly Church of England agenda in its religious output. The day kicks off with *Prayer for the Day*, transmitted at 5.43 a.m., except on Sunday, when the *Bells on Sunday* are broadcast from a different church at that same time, followed on long wave by *Sunday Worship*. In addition, Radio 4 marks significant moments in the liturgical calendar with programmes such as *Midnight Mass* (at Christmas), *Lent Talks* and *Good Friday Liturgy*.

But that is not to say that people of all faiths (and none) are not catered for. In fact, quite the reverse is true, and agnostics, atheists, Bahá'is, Buddhists, Hindus, humanists, Jews, Muslims, pagans, Sikhs and many others have all been invited to air their views and discuss their faith over the airwaves.

In a reorganisation in 2000, the Religious Broadcasting Department was renamed Religion and Ethics. It was said that the powers that be were more into 'New Age stuff' than traditional religious output. The early retirement the following year of the Head of Religious Broadcasting, the Revd Ernie Rea, alarmed the Church of England, and was thought to be a comment on the downgrading of religious programming.

A LITTLE 4 THOUGHT

In 2011 Radio 4 celebrated the 400th anniversary of the King James Bible by devoting an entire Sunday to readings from that version.

BEYOND BELIEF

PROGRAMME STATS

Running since: 2002

Current presenter: The Revd Ernie Rea

Description: Series exploring the place and nature of faith in today's world.

Website: www.bbc.co.uk/programmes/b006s6p6

Typically, a half-hour episode of *Beyond Belief* features a panel of four representatives from different (or no) religious traditions plus presenter Ernie Rea.

Occasionally, the guests have a similar outlook. A 2012 programme looking into 'new atheism', for example, provided a forum for three guests who broadly identified themselves as atheists.

Between them, the guests discuss the religious aspects of a vast range of topics. Past discussions have included the environment, Stonehenge, yoga, the Pope, creation, the law, monogamy, funeral methods and animal ethics – life, in fact, along with the universe and everything in it.

A LITTLE ④ THOUGHT

For three years Ernie Rea served as a Presbyterian minister on the Shankill Road in Belfast – the heart of the Northern Ireland 'Troubles'.

❝ *It's a sort of ecumenical love-in.* **❞**
**THE REVD DR PETER MULLEN IN *THE TELEGRAPH*,
24 APRIL 2012**

THOUGHT FOR THE DAY

PROGRAMME STATS

Running since: 1970

Website: www.bbc.co.uk/programmes/p00szxv6/clips

Twitter: @thought4theday

There has been a breakfast-time spiritual reflection slot on the Home Service/Radio 4 since 1939, when *Lift Up Your Hearts* was first broadcast. Exclusively Christian in content, it continued until 1965, when an interfaith version, *Ten to Eight*, was introduced. This transferred to Radio 4, until it was replaced by *Thought for the Day* in 1970.

Belying its size, *Thought for the Day* packs a powerful punch as a controversial programme that often touches on sensitivities – some religious and others political.

These days, roughly four in five *Thought for the Day* contributors are Christian, with, for example, a Sikh, Jewish or Muslim representative invited to contribute every fifth or sixth programme.

Thought for the Day has long been a battleground for the 'religious versus secular' debate, with the National Secular Society claiming that 'the BBC devotes too much of its resources to the provision of religious propaganda, funded by the licence payer'.

For all the BBC's apparent intransigence, however, on a couple of occasions there has been a flash of secularism on *Thought for the Day*. The first occurred in 2002, when career atheist Richard Dawkins was permitted to present a secular *Thought for the Day*, although not at the usual time – the 7.45 a.m. 'God slot' apparently being considered sacred.

Then, when he was guest editor of the Boxing Day 2013 *Today* programme, Sir Tim Berners-Lee wanted to invite an atheist minister from the Unitarian Church, Andrew Pakula, to present *Thought for the Day*. In the end a compromise was reached whereby Pakula was permitted to deliver an *Alternative Thought for the Day* an hour earlier. Introducing him, presenter Mishal Husain explained that *TftD* 'is part of the BBC's religious programming and is a reflection by speakers from the perspective of their faith'.

The balance was redressed an hour after Pakula's reflection, when a theistic Unitarian minister delivered *TftD* at the usual time. Later on *Today*, Justin Webb wryly observed that the world had not stopped spinning.

SOME *TFTD* RADICALS

In 1971, one of the regular contributors, Methodist minister the Revd Dr Colin Morris, criticised the Conservative Party's immigration policy as unchristian. His comments outraged the party whips and led to questions being asked in the House of Lords. After a brief spell away he returned to *TftD* until 2009.

In 1990, at the height of the poll tax controversy, it came to the producers' attention that regular contributor (and Chaplain to the Queen) Canon Eric James was intending to talk about 'the spiritual value of revolt'. He was urged to change his script, refused and resigned, later claiming in *Church Times* that he had faced censorship.

A LITTLE 4 THOUGHT

On 29 March 2014 *Thought for the Day* was delivered by the Revd Geraldine Granger, aka the Vicar of Dibley, aka Dawn French as part of Radio 4's Character Invasion Day.

In 1988, regular *TftD* contributor Rabbi Lionel Blue chose 'Why Has a Cow Got Four Legs?' by Cicely Courtneidge as his favourite *Desert Island Disc*. He explained that the song has a metaphysical element.

SUNDAY

PROGRAMME STATS

Running since: 1990

Current presenters: Ed Stourton, along with Jane Little, William Crawley and Samira Ahmed

Past presenters: Roger Bolton, Chris Morgan

Description: The religious and ethical news of the week.

Website: www.bbc.co.uk/programmes/b006qnbd

Twitter: @BBCR4Sunday

A typical *Sunday* packs a whole lot into 45 minutes. As an example, here's what was broadcast on Sunday 1, June 2014:

Ed Stourton talks to the brother-in-law of a woman jailed for apostasy in Sudan, and asks how she is coping following the birth of her daughter.

Can the Church of England 'compete' Wonga out of business?

The religious implications in the upcoming Syrian elections.

The Assisted Dying Bill is discussed by a rabbi and the Executive Officer of Right to Life.

Three new musical settings of the Stabat Mater.

Ten years after the launch of the Street Pastors (an interdenominational response to urban problems), Trevor Barnes goes out on a night patrol in Brixton with the movement's founder.

SOMETHING UNDERSTOOD

PROGRAMME STATS

Running since: 1995

Current presenter: Mark Tully

Past presenters: Joan Bakewell, Bonnie Greer, Fergal Keane, Sheena McDonald

Description: Ethical and religious discussion that examines some of the larger questions of life, taking a spiritual theme and exploring it through music, prose and poetry.

Website: www.bbc.co.uk/programmes/b006qn7f

In 2012, shortly before he retired as Archbishop of Canterbury, Rowan Williams was interviewed on *Something Understood*, considering whether 'discretion is the better part of valour'.

In February 2013 a special edition of the programme featured the Dalai Lama, interviewed in the Ladakh region of India, talking about the mind.

> 66 *Church-bells beyond the stars heard,*
> *the soul's blood,*
> *The land of spices; something understood.* 99
> **GEORGE HERBERT (1593–1633), FROM 'PRAYER'**

ETHICS ON RADIO 4

MORAL MAZE

PROGRAMME STATS

Running since: 1990

Current presenter: Michael Buerk

Description: Combative, provocative and engaging live debate examining the moral issues behind one of the week's news stories.

Website: www.bbc.co.uk/programmes/b006qk11

Twitter: #moralmaze

Believe it or not, when the strand was first devised it was hoped that the format would encourage panellists to change their minds during the course of the programme. Of course the opposite often ended up being the case, with people becoming more entrenched in their views.

Four guest 'witnesses' are cross-examined by four of the regular panellists, in a format that roughly reflects the procedures of a

Select Committee in Westminster. The panel debate the moral and ethical issues arising from a news story. It is said that it is required listening for Westminster MPs, to keep them up to date with the hot topics of the day.

MORAL MAZE PANELLISTS

Regular *Moral Maze* panellists include Ann McElvoy of *The Economist* and former Conservative Cabinet member Michael Portillo, along with:

Claire Fox – a libertarian known for being outspoken and often outrageous. In the past she has been associated with Trotskyism, Marxism and the Revolutionary Communist Party. She founded the Institute of Ideas, to create a public space where ideas can be contested without constraint.

Giles Fraser – an Anglican priest, journalist and 'controversialist'. He founded Inclusive Church, which campaigns for gay and lesbian inclusion within the Church. In 2011, when he was Canon Chancellor of St Paul's Cathedral, he opposed the forced removal of the Occupy London protestors who were camped outside the cathedral. It led to his resignation.

Kenan Malik – a science historian who campaigns for equal rights, freedom of expression, a secular society, rationalism and humanism in the face of what he sees as a growing culture of irrationalism, mysticism and misanthropy.

Melanie Phillips – social commentator for the *Daily Mail*. She started on the left of the political spectrum, writing for *The Guardian* and *New Statesman*. During the 1990s, however, she moved to the right, in her own words from being a 'darling of the left to champion of the moral high ground'.

Matthew Taylor – a former Labour councillor. In 2006 he became chief executive of the Royal Society for the Encouragement of Arts, Manufactures and Commerce, an organisation committed to finding practical solutions to today's social challenges.

THINGS YOU (PROBABLY) NEVER KNEW ABOUT MICHAEL BUERK

His initial hopes of going into the RAF were dashed by poor eyesight. After briefly working as a hod-carrier on a building site, he took up a career in journalism because it sounded 'trendy and bohemian'.

After ninety-nine out of a hundred job applications to newspapers were rejected, he was finally taken on by the *Bromsgrove Messenger* because, as he says, he and the editor had a shared interest in cricket.

One of his first journalism jobs, working for the *Daily Mail*, involved tracking George Best's movements around the nightclubs of Manchester.

His uncompromising reporting on the apartheid regime resulted in his expulsion from South Africa in 1987.

In 2013 *Michael Buerk: The Newsical* had a three-night run at the Network Theatre in Waterloo. Billed as 'The untold and mostly untrue story of 80s news icon Michael Buerk', it portrayed a love affair between him and Moira Stuart (who gets pregnant), and featured 'evil weather genius Ian McCaskill'. The critics panned it as 'a very bad piece of theatre'.

THE DEBATES

Some of the topics covered by *Moral Maze* in March 2014:

Is our obsession with class a sign of a sense of fairness, or a prejudice to be fought?

How do we use the law when there's a conflict between individual liberty and social norms?

Morality and principle in foreign policy.

What are the moral underpinnings of nationalism?

What are the limits of science when it comes to making moral and ethical choices?

When should the common good outweigh our freedom to do as we please?

Are sporting boycotts of events like the Winter Olympics effective or just empty gestures?

Portrait of the Presenter As a Listener
MICHAEL BUERK
Presenter, *Moral Maze*

My first memory of Radio 4 is... hiding behind the sofa at home listening to *Journey into Space* on the Home Service in the 50s. There was always something horrible, but chillingly undefined, in the airlock. I was terrified. Now the only thing that terrifies me on Radio 4 is Jenni Murray.

When I'm not working I'm listening to... Radio 4, of course. I will even listen to *You and Yours*, if necessary. There is no more telling sign of Radio 4 addiction.

Radio 4 matters because... it is one of the last corners of the media world aimed consistently at reasonably educated, reasonably intelligent grown-ups. It is one thing the BBC does that will never be done by a commercial station, or at least not done to the same standard. As far as I know it has no rival anywhere.

INSIDE THE ETHICS COMMITTEE
PROGRAMME STATS

Running since: 2005

Presenters: Vivienne Parry, Joan Bakewell

Description: A panel of experts discuss real-life cases to explore the workings of clinical ethics committees.

Website: www.bbc.co.uk/programmes/b007xbtd

At the heart of the programme are some really heart-rending stories. The listener listens with a sense of 'there but for the grace of God go I'. Yet the programme manages to tread the very fine line between sentimentality and being too matter-of-fact in tone – a difficult feat when your reason for looking at a real-life story is to dissect it and examine it closely for the general ethical principles contained within it.

Each programme outlines the case study, before the presenter discusses it with a panel of experts. Series 9 covered topics such as:

How much should a seriously ill seventeen-year-old know about his condition and its prognosis?

Should a mother be allowed to have her children tested for a life-threatening faulty gene?

What happens when Muslim beliefs are at odds with medical decisions?

Should a woman with severe disabilities be helped to get pregnant?

> 66 *The twists and shifts in this tale…*
> *left you feeling seasick.* 99
> **ELISABETH MAHONEY IN *THE GUARDIAN*, 14 JULY 2011**

TAKING A STAND

This series ran between 2007 and 2010, and in each programme Fergal Keane talked to people who through conviction or circumstance had been forced to take a stand or make sacrifices for what they believe in.

Some of the stories are extraordinary, some are disturbing, others frankly the stuff of nightmares.

Among Keane's interviewees were:

Suzanne Hook, who founded an orphanage in Vietnam.

Jean-Robert Cadet, a former Haitian child slave.

Claudia Wallace, whose brother Hugo was kidnapped.

André Hanscombe, whose partner Rachel Nickell was murdered in 1992.

Barbara Harris, whose organisation pays addicted women to take contraception.

Dr Jim Swire, whose daughter, Flora, died in the Lockerbie bombing.

Peter Stapleton, who was attacked by Somali pirates.

Chinese businessman Jimmy Lai, who supported the Tiananmen Square protesters in 1989.

Garry Kasparov on being a dissenting voice in Russian politics.

Paul Kelly, whose eighteen-year-old son Simon killed himself.

Identical twins who were separated at birth as part of an experiment.

SPORT ON 4

A SPORTING CHANCE

In the early days of BBC Radio, because of agreements with the newspapers, no live commentary of sports events was permitted. When the 1926 Derby was transmitted live, for example, listeners could hear the thunder of horses' hooves and the cheers of the crowd, but had to wait until the 7 p.m. news bulletin to find out who had won. Shortly afterwards, however, all that changed, and 1927 was a bonanza year for sports fans. Here are the fixtures which made it first past the post with live commentary:

22 January   Arsenal v. Sheffield United from Highbury becomes the first football to be broadcast on BBC Radio.

25 March   The Grand National is broadcast from Aintree.

2 April   The Boat Race is broadcast.

23 April   The FA Cup Final – Cardiff v. Arsenal – is broadcast from Wembley Stadium (1–0 to Cardiff).

14 May   The first cricket commentary is New Zealand v. Essex. (It was not considered a success, and ball-by-ball commentary was not introduced until 1938.)

SPORT ON FOUR

Sport on Four was a long-running Radio 4 programme that aired on Saturday morning between 1977 and 1998. Its original presenter was Welsh cricketer Tony Lewis.

When Lewis left the programme in 1986 to commentate on television cricket, *Sport on Four* had a series of guest presenters, including Chris Brasher, Harry Carpenter, David Coleman, Des Lynam, Ron Pickering and others.

Eventually Cliff Morgan took over the presenter's role in 1987 and remained at the helm until 1998, when it was replaced in the new schedule by John Peel's *Home Truths*.

SPORT TODAY ON RADIO 4

These days, if you want to tune into a game or match you have to tune into Radio 5 Live – apart, of course, from *Test Match Special* (more on that shortly). But Radio 4 is by no means a sport-free zone:

If you want to know about women and sport, *Woman's Hour* interviews many of the sportswomen who are in the news, while Kelly Holmes was invited to guest-edit a whole episode in 2014.

If technology is your thing, in the run-up to the London Olympics Chris Ledgard presented *The Gizmo Games*, a fascinating insight into the intelligence, espionage, radar-tracking technology, wireless body sensors and missile identification lasers that were used during the Games.

Leading up to 2012, Peter White presented *Children of the Olympic Bid*, which followed the progress of the youngsters who had helped to secure the Olympics for London in Singapore.

If you're looking for a historical perspective, *Hunt/Lauda* (2013) was a fascinating insight into the relationship between Formula One drivers James Hunt and Niki Lauda.

A LITTLE **4** THOUGHT

Olympic Arts, a programme aired in 2008, told the story of the Pentathlon of the Muses. Broadcaster Mark Whitaker revealed that, as part of the Games between 1912 and 1948, medals were awarded for architecture, painting, sculpture, literature and music.

TEST MATCH SPECIAL

PROGRAMME STATS

Running since: 1957 (1994 on Radio 4 LW)

Current time slots: When the cricket's on

Current presenters: Jonathan Agnew, Henry Blofeld

Past presenters include: John Arlott, Robert Hudson, Brian Johnston, Christopher Martin-Jenkins, Don Mosey

Description: International cricket.

Website: www.bbc.co.uk/programmes/b00c67t1

If you think Blowers, Aggers, Johnners and Tuffers are types of pond life, this section is probably not for you. Similarly, feminists who want to see better representation of women in broadcasting are also advised to skip this section – the focus of which is the unapologetic boys' club that is *Test Match Special.*

Originally on Radio 3 medium wave, then on Radio 5, *TMS* found its present home on Radio 4 LW when 5 Live was launched with a schedule of sports and news that didn't allow for the variable length of cricket games.

Test Match Special isn't just about test match cricket. It also encompasses county games, one-dayers and Twenty20 matches. And that, in itself, seems an apt introduction to *TMS*. Because in this age of rigid definitions, it simply doesn't do 'what it says on the tin', and in our culture of schedules and deadlines, it rambles defiantly around the airwaves for 6, 7 or 8 hours at a time – a law unto itself that answers to only one thing – the rain.

Within that loose framework the commentators, summarisers, scorers and guests apparently amble through the broadcast, making it up as they go along, munching cake and somehow making the most unremarkable observations about pigeons and cranes seem entertaining. They defy all the rules of good broadcasting – and we love them the more for it. Above all, of course, we love the innuendo and the way that Aggers genuinely doesn't appear to realise what he's just said about putting on a rubber.

This banal-yet-somehow-entertaining drivel can go on for hours in the background – the half-listened-to soundtrack to which people up and down the country are getting on with things around the home or driving to their destinations. But then, just when you have become lulled into the world of cooing pigeons, rumbling buses, casual sexism and cake, something happens on the field.

As one enthusiast put it:

It goes on like a happily babbling brook in the background. It could be a five-day game when not a lot happens and you're waiting for a team to declare or a match is petering out to a draw. Then suddenly something kicks off. It could be a game-changer, like when Flintoff ran out Ponting in 2009 and turned the Ashes upside down. And then you realise with a jolt that they're not quite as stupefied by cake as they might seem, and like dogs after a scent they're off – and you just go with them.

Chris Goddard, cricket fan

A LITTLE 4 THOUGHT

Apparently the now-common cake gag started quite literally as a gag – when someone handed Johnners a slice, followed quickly by the microphone. Ever since then the listening public has been inundating the box with cakes of all shapes and sizes.

BOYCOTT BINGO

You can find Boycott bingo cards on the Internet and then, when Boycott utters one of his immortal phrases, you cross it off your card. Here are some examples:

'Could have hit that with a stick of rhubarb.'
'No more brains than a pork pie.'
'Should book in for bed and breakfast on this wicket.'
'Batting's all about grafting.'
'Me mum could have caught that in her pinny.'

A SPOT OF LUNCH

Ever the gentleman, Aggers always likes to entertain a lunch guest, particularly if it's Lily Allen. He must do a very good lunch, because the A-listers queue up to accept his invitation.

Guests have included: Heston Blumenthal, Ken Bruce, Eric Clapton, Ken Clarke, Alice Cooper, Hugh Cornwell, Tom Courtenay, Russell Crowe, Stephen Fry, Hugh Grant, Roy Hodgson, Elton John, Miles Jupp, Ian Lavender, Michael McIntyre, Ed Miliband, David Mitchell, Annie Nightingale, Michael Palin, Nicholas Parsons, Daniel Radcliffe (on his eighteenth birthday). Oh, and did we mention Lily Allen?

A LITTLE  THOUGHT

On one occasion when rain delayed the start of the afternoon session, Brian Johnston ended up chatting to actor Bill Pertwee for an hour and a half after lunch.

The calypso *TMS* music is 'Soul Limbo' by Booker T and the MGs.

BRIAN JOHNSTON (1912–1994)

Johnners originally wanted to be an actor but was persuaded to enter the family coffee business instead. In 1939 he joined the 2nd Battalion Grenadier Guards, where he served as a Technical Adjutant and was awarded the Military Cross.

After the war he joined the BBC, intending to stay for only a few months. His first broadcasts were live radio programmes from music halls and theatres. Between 1948 and 1952 he made his name with the live feature 'Let's Go Somewhere' on the popular Saturday night radio programme *In Town Tonight*.

In 1963 he became the BBC's first cricket correspondent. After he was dropped by BBC Television 'for being too humorous', in 1970 he transferred to radio, where he became a national institution.

All in all, those 'few months' at the BBC turned into a total of forty-eight years.

A LITTLE 4 THOUGHT

In the early days of his career Johnners used to perform stunts. According to the website dedicated to him (www.johnners.com), these included staying alone in the Chamber of Horrors, riding a circus horse, lying under a train, being hauled out of the sea by a helicopter and being attacked by a police dog.

CHRISTOPHER MARTIN-JENKINS
(1945–2013)

CMJ, as he was affectionately known, was a keen cricketer from his schoolboy days, and became captain of the First XI when he was at prep school.

He was clearly bitten by the bug, because he wrote to Brian Johnston to ask how he could follow in his path. Johnners took him out to lunch and told him to keep playing and watching cricket, and to practise speaking into a tape recorder.

At Cambridge University CMJ had more success at rugby than cricket. He did, however, captain the University Second XI in 1966 and 1967, as well as his college XI. After university he played one Second XI Championship match for Surrey against Warwickshire at the Oval in 1971, and appeared for the Sir Paul Getty XI between 1992 and 2002, with a final appearance at the age of sixty-one against the Tim Rice's Heartaches team.

CMJ joined *TMS* in 1972, and remained part of the team for every home season for the next thirty-eight years.

During his career he was the first non-professional cricketer to be invited to give the annual MCC Cowdrey address, and in 2010 he became President of the MCC.

A LITTLE 4 THOUGHT

On one occasion at Cambridge, Christopher Martin-Jenkins played cricket alongside Henry Blofeld, when CMJ was co-opted to make up the numbers for the alumni side in their annual fixture against the University First XI.

A TIMELINE OF GAFFES AND GIGGLES

According to Johnners, one of his earliest gaffes was a spoonerism when he was attempting to say that Hampshire cricketer Henry Horton looked as though he was 'sitting on a shooting stick'. It was the beginning of a distinguished career in gaffe-making:

1961, Headingley: 'There's Neil Harvey standing at leg slip with his legs wide apart, waiting for a tickle.'

1969, Lord's: When New Zealand batsman Glenn Turner collapsed after being hit in the box and lay writhing on the ground, it fell to Johnners to waffle on, pretending that Turner had been hit anywhere except where he had. After a few minutes Turner got up, looking a little pale but determined to carry on. Johnners remarked how plucky Turner was and breezily announced: 'One ball left.'

1976, The Oval: The famous quote 'The bowler's Holding, the batsman's Willey' referred to Michael Holding of the West Indies and Peter Willey of England. Johnston claimed he was only alerted to what he'd said later, when he received a letter of complaint from a lady listener.

1991, The Oval: Aggers suggested that Botham was out because he had failed to 'get his leg over'. Johnners attempted to carry on commentating for half a minute before both of them dissolved into paroxysms of laughter.

> **❝** *Radio 4 means sitting in my partner's parents' house, listening to the cricket for hours and hours trying to do a jigsaw or crossword or sudoku – chill-out time after hiking the hills in Ireland.* **❞**
> **NICKY WOOD, INFORMATION CENTRE SUPERVISOR**

LETTER FROM AMERICA

There is one programme from the archives that deserves a special mention – and it seems appropriate to round off this Radio 4 miscellany with a nod in its direction.

It was a weekly fifteen-minute series broadcast first on the Home Service and then on Radio 4. It ran for a breathtaking 2,869 programmes spanning fifty-eight years – from March 1946 to February 2004 – and holds the record as the longest-running speech programme in radio history.

Letter from America was actually a neat reversal of a programme Alistair Cooke had broadcast from London before moving to the United States. As NBC's London correspondent, each week he would record *London Letter*, a fifteen-minute broadcast about life in Britain. His broadcasts from London covered all aspects of life, including the abdication of Edward VIII in 1936.

In 1937, when Cooke and his first wife Ruth moved to New York, he suggested to the BBC the idea of doing *London Letter* in reverse. *Mainly about Manhattan* ran for a short while, but after nineteen episodes the idea was shelved at the outbreak of war.

When Cooke resumed his broadcasts after the war, his programmes witnessed the years when America was in the ascendancy as a superpower, and when events that happened stateside were invariably of enormous global significance:

In 1968 he was just yards away from where Robert Kennedy was assassinated.

He reported on Richard Nixon's disgrace and resignation in 1974.

In 1977 he commented on the death of Elvis (although he never did get the rock and roll thing).

Letter from America is perhaps the ultimate audio blog and, like all good bloggers, Cooke knew that his words were intended for an audience rather than being the product of a mere navel-gazing exercise. When he did resort to self-reflection, he did so in such a way that the listener could relate to his sentiments.

Being pieces based on the personality of its writer and presenter, *Letter from America* could never have survived without its auteur, Cooke. He retired from his other jobs in 1992, but continued to present *Letter* for a further twelve years. At the age of ninety-five, in early March 2004, he announced his retirement from *Letter from America*. He died four weeks later at his home in New York.

Upon hearing of his death, there were surely many listeners who, already bereft of their regular fix of his voice – the soothing, avuncular tones which were wrapped like cotton wool around razor-sharp insight and wry humour – echoed the sentiment Cooke himself expressed when a hero of his died: 'Duke Ellington died last week. I don't have to believe it if I don't want to.'

A LITTLE ④ THOUGHT

Until 1950 *Letter from America* was titled *American Letter*.

A POST SCRIPT

In 2004, the BBC published many of *Letter from America*'s transcripts, and nearly 3,000 scripts have been made available in an electronic archive administered by the University of East Anglia.

In 2012, the BBC made over 900 episodes available in full online, and in 2014 it was announced that a further 650 editions had been recovered that were previously thought to be lost. Most of these had been recorded by two listeners – Roy Whittaker and David Henderson – and stored variously in a cellar, an attic and a fertiliser spreader for nearly forty years.

SELECT BIBLIOGRAPHY

Brooke-Taylor, Tim; Garden, Graeme; Cryer, Barry; Lyttelton, Humphrey: *The Little Book of Mornington Crescent* (2000, Orion)

Clarke, Nick: *Alistair Cooke: A Biography* (2000, Arcade)

Dillon, Rosie: *The Archers: An Unofficial Companion* (2011, Summersdale)

Donovan, Paul: *The Radio Companion* (1991, HarperCollins)

Elmes, Simon: *And Now on Radio 4* (2007, Arrow)

Hendy, David: *Life on Air: A History of Radio 4* (2007, OUP)

Stuart, Charles (ed.): *The Reith Diaries* (1975, Collins)

ACKNOWLEDGEMENTS

My thanks go to the many Radio 4 buffs who have shared their must-listens and pet hates with me, in particular the presenters, politicians and Pargetters who have taken the time to give me their first-hand stories as Radio 4 listeners: Hilary Benn MP, Michael Buerk, Alison Dowling, Shaun Ley, Caroline Lucas MP, Paddy O'Connell, Nicholas Parsons, Michael Portillo, Libby Purves, Eric Robson and Ritula Shah.

Thanks also go to the Radio 4 Communications Team for fielding my queries, to Steve Arnold of the *Radio Times* Archive (www.radiotimesarchive.co.uk), to Dean Bedford of *Just a Minute* Statistics (www.just-a-minute.info), to Abbie Headon and Abi McMahon of Summersdale for their suggestions and support and to Ray Hamilton for his meticulous and thorough editing.

Above all to Chris, for his unstinting support, patience and additional research. I cannot really take credit for any of the section on *Test Match Special*.

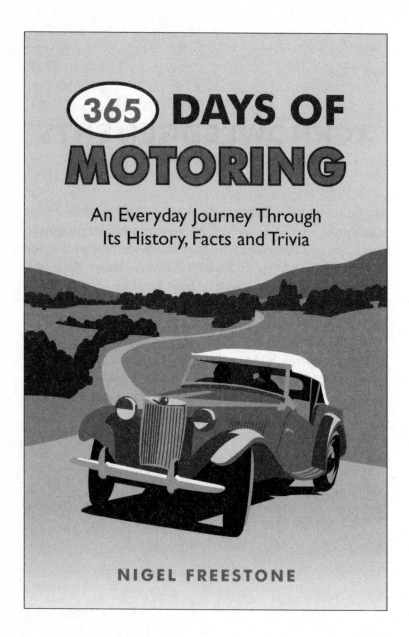

365 DAYS OF MOTORING

An Everyday Journey Through Its History, Facts and Trivia

NIGEL FREESTONE

365 DAYS OF MOTORING

An Everyday Journey Through Its History, Facts and Trivia

Nigel Freestone

£9.99

Hardback

ISBN: 978-1-84953-654-7

2 February

1898: The first four-wheeled automobile, an imported Panhard et Levassor, was driven Japan.

1954: The legendary Ford Thunderbird was launched at the Detroit Auto Show.

2004: A standard 2004 Dodge Ram SRT-10, driven by NASCAR driver Brendan Gaughan (USA), reached a speed of 248.783 km/h (154.587 mph) at the Daimler Chrysler Proving Grounds in Chelsea, Michigan, USA, to establish a new speed record for production pickup trucks.

Belt up and enjoy this 365-day ride as you cruise past the most momentous motoring events in history.

Packed with fascinating facts about races, motorists and the history of the mighty engine, this book is a must-have for any car enthusiast.

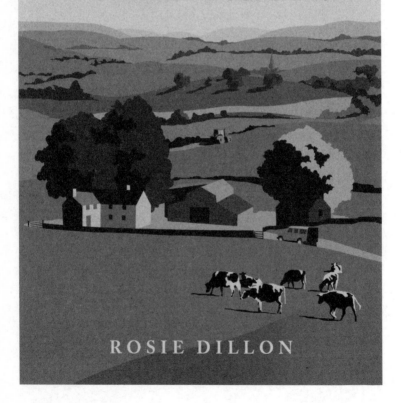

The Archers

AN UNOFFICIAL COMPANION

ROSIE DILLON

THE ARCHERS
An Unofficial Companion

Rosie Dillon

£9.99
Hardback
ISBN: 978-1-84953-178-8

Who are Jean-Paul, Baggy, Mercedes and Rhys?

When did Susan Carter hit the headlines as the 'Ambridge One'?

Which teatime treat delighted Camilla, Duchess of Cornwall, on her visit to the village?

It's been sixty years since the familiar dum-di-dum-di-dum-di-dum of 'Barwick Green' first brought The Archers to our airwaves, and in that time millions of listeners have eavesdropped on the dramas of Ambridge life.

This fascinating compendium, which brings together facts about characters, controversies and country customs, along with quizzes to test even the keenest listener, is sure to delight avid addicts and nervous newbies alike.

If you're interested in finding out more about our books,
find us on Facebook at **Summersdale Publishers** and
follow us on Twitter at **@Summersdale**.

www.summersdale.com